Summer of 1940, during the Battle of Britain, with ground crews sighting the guns on F/O 'Watty' Watson's Hurricane P2829. Note the typical non-standard fuselage roundel and the red area of the tail flash painted to the leading edge of the tail.

Hurricane Squadron

No 87 Squadron at War 1939–1941

by Perry Adams

AIR
RESEARCH
·PUBLICATIONS·

First published 1988

ISBN 1 871187 00 1

Typeset by Qualitext, Salisbury SP2 7BE and printed in England by Oxford University Press, Walton Street, Oxford OX2 6AB, for the publishers Air Research Publications, 34 Elm Road, New Malden, Surrey KT3 3HD.
Produced by Kristall Productions Ltd, 71b Maple Road, Surbiton, Surrey KT6 4AG.

In the late 1970s, a former member of the 87 Squadron, 'Danny' Daniels, took upon himself the task of contacting as many of the 'Old Boys' as he could. He was successful in finding over 60 and has organised regular reunions ever since. It is largely as a result of these gatherings that I have been able to gather the material included in this book and for that I must extend my heartfelt gratitude to all who have tolerated this 'young chap' and extended many a helping hand in the form of photographs and boundless enthusiasm. Whilst compiling the material and researching the story of No 87 Squadron has been a most rewarding and fascinating task, it has also been tinged with sadness for me as several of the men who had become personal friends sadly passed away.

Perry Adams.

One of the perks of writing this book. 'Rubber' Thorogood, Author, Jack Harding and 'Dimmy' Joyce enjoy a drink at the 1984 reunion (Watson).

Right: The He 111 shot down by F/O Vose-Jeff was the first enemy aircraft to be brought down by RAF fighters in France. Dennis David peers into the cockpit. The crew were taken to a French hospital where they were neglected by their captors, but when Vose-Jeff visited them he ensured that the correct treatment was accorded them (Guppy).

The dramatic night intruder attack by 'Widge' Gleed (flying LK-A) and 'Roddy' 'Raynor on Carpiquet airfield near Caen on March 14, 1941, graphically described by Gleed on page 41. Painting by Mark Postlethwaite.

Flight Lieutenant 'Widge' Gleed in his Hurricane, the famous LK-A, with the Disney character Figaro the Cat painted on the cockpit door panel.

Foreword

by Wing Commander R. P. Beamont, CBE, DSO, DFC, DL, FRAeS

In the spring of 1940, four Hurricane squadrons faced the might of Hitler's Luftwaffe as it was unleashed in the all-out attack by Germany on France and Belgium on the 10 May. These squadrons formed the fighter element of the Air Component of the British Expeditionary Force (the BEF) which was charged with holding the line between the French held Maginot Line and the Belgian frontier.

With dramatic speed, which has now become part of the history of war, the German Blitzkreig swung across neutral Belgium and by-passed the French entirely in their Maginot 'strongholds'; and within 10 days the Panzer armoured spearheads were threatening the French channel ports.

With brilliant foresight, but agonizing decision, the Commander-in-Chief of Fighter Command resisted all pressures to send the home-based Hurricane and Spitfire squadrons to France to try and stemp the tide. He retained all the Spitfires for home defence and allowed only a few extra Hurrican squadrons to move forward to French airfields on daily reinforcements, returning to the UK each night. These and the four 'permanent' Hurricane squadrons met such intense action that detailed records could often not be kept, and it was not until they were withdrawn to home bases after the 20 May, 1940, by which time, it could be seen that the battle was already lost on the ground, that the cost could be counted.

No. 87 Squadron, the subject of this diary account, research with dedication by Perry Adams, returned to Church Fenton via Debden with seven of it's original sixteen aircraft, having lost nine pilots killed and five wounded in the 10 days fighting; but in that short time they have claimed more than 80 victories!

Subsequent assessments of the French campaign and the later Battle of Britain have shown that the actual enemy losses were seldom more than half those claimed and often much less, and that this tendency to over-claim in the excitement of the moment existed on both sides. Nevertheless No. 87 Squadron's claim of 80 plus victories demonstrated that their Hurricanes had fired their guns at at least 80 enemy targets in that fierce ten days — an intensity of air-fighting that had not been thought of in the early months of the coming battles now seen to be inevitable over the Channel and, if we could not stop them there, over our own homeland.

With just one month at Church Fenton to re-equip with new Hurricanes and start the operational training of replacement pilots, No. 87 Squadron was ready again to face the Luftwaffe across the Channel in the South West and soon they came. First in small formations to attack convoys off Portland and Plymouth, and then with rapidly increasing ferocity in July and early August until raids of 150 plus became the norm against major targets like Portland Naval base, Southampton and Bristol.

In the summer of 1940, at the height of the Battle of Britain, P/O Roddy Rayner is framed by the undercarriage of his Hurricane as he prepares for a sortie

The story of the defence of the British Isles against the might of the German Air Force in 1940 is an established saga in the history of modern warfare, and the tales of the Spitfire and Hurricane squadrons and their pilots make entrhalling reading. At 1 August 1940, 650 Hurricanes and Spitfires, in a ratio of 2 to 1 in 52 RAF Squadrons, stood against 2,700 fighters and bombers of Hitler's skilled, determined and seemingly victorious Luftwaffe.

No. 87 Squadron was one of those squadrons, and author Perry Adams has put together a remarkable tribute to the pilots and ground crews who, like all their colleagues in Fighter Command, stood firm and took on the invading enemy wherever he could be found. They did this without bravado and with a matter of fact approach which was perhaps a classic example of the character of this race in adversity.

No-one who served in a fighter squadron at that time will ever forget how even the most desperate days were met with an almost casual 'this is what we are here for, so let's get on with it' attitude.

No. 87 which was there at the beginning in France, lost two squadron commanders, five flight commanders and more than half its pilot complement, before the Battle of Britain ended in victory.

Its members believed that theirs was the finest of all fighter squadrons as did all the members of all the other fighter squadrons and that was and is RAF morale.

R. P. Beamont

The First No. 87 Squadron

From its formation in September 1917, No 87 Squadron was intended to be a fighter squadron. 'D' Squadron of the Central Flying School at Upavon provided the nucleus of men and aircraft which were a mixed bag of Avro 504Ks, Sopwith Pups and SE 5As. By December, the squadron had moved to Hounslow, where they re-equipped with Sopwith Dolphins, which they ferried to France as replacement machines for the Dolphin squadrons stationed there. It was not until April 1918, that the squadron went to France to take part in operations themselves.

Inititally coastal patrols were flown extending as far as Zeebrugge, in Belguim. Then they were given the specific task of intercepting German high altitude reconnaissance aircraft and within 10 days they had succeeded in destroying eight of them. With the opening of the British offensive in July, the squadron turned its attention to fighter patrols and ground attack missions. For this, the squadron armourers remounted the twin Lewis guns on the lower mainplane, thus a greater volume of fire could be brought to bear on troops and other ground targets. The arrangement was also suited to fighter combat as, on 21 August, the squadron claimed the destruction of 10 enemy aircraft. During the short time that they were engaged in operations, 89 enemy aircraft were claimed as destroyed or shot down out of control.

Following the armistice the squadron returned to England, to Ternhill, where they were officially disbanded on 24 June 1919. So ended the first No 87 Squadron, but the growing concern about the situation in Europe fired an expansion of the RAF in the late 1930s and, on 15 March 1937, No 87 Squadron was reformed at Tangmere. At first the squadron was equipped with Hawker Furies, and then Gladiators, before a move was made to Debden, where the squadron re-equipped with the new eight gun fighter, the Hawker Hurricane.

L1648, attached to No 85 Squadron. which overshot when landing at Debden on October 6, 1938. The ortho film used for this picture makes the yellow outer of the roundel appear dark (Guppy).

1. The Phoney War

When war was declared, on 3 September 1939, No 87 Squadron had a total of 12 operational aircraft and pilots based at Debden, some 40 miles north of London. These were split into two flights, known as 'A' and 'B' Flights, which were kept operational by 80 groundcrew.

In the years leading up to the outbreak of war, it was speculated that an attack of devastating scale would take place with days, if not hours, of the declaration of war. Fearing an imminent attack, the squadron began to fly night patrols. On 4 September, with the war only hours old, 'B' Flight was ordered to intercept three 'enemy aircraft' which proved to have been a false alarm and Pilot Officer St John crash-landed his Hurricane, which was severely damaged. On 6 September, another night interception resulted in the discovery of six RAF Blenheims approaching the coast and once more the frustrated pilots returned to Debden.

Only six days after the declaration of war news reached the squadron that they were to move immediately to an airfield in France, known as Merville. They were to join Nos 1, 73 and 85 Squadrons and fly in support of the British Expeditionary Force.

Merville, it was found, was a town situated in Northern France, not far from the Belgian border, and the airfield to which the Hurricane pilots arrived consisted of no more than a grass strip. To make the place even less appealing, the airfield was often water logged and as aircraft touched down, sheets of spray were sent high into the air making them seem more like flying boats!

It took less than an hour to fly from Debden to Merville, but the groundcrews took two days to make the journey. Sergeant Francis Pecket, an airframe fitter, had been with the squadron since 1937 and still recalls his part in the move.

"We, the ground crews, had a tiresome journey. The day started by train to a Channel port for a ferry trip to Cherbourg, we then had a long route march from the docks to the railway station where we began the third leg. The carriages which we were using were very uncomfortable and, with all the squadron crammed in, it was impossible to get any kind of sleep. During the trip across Northern France, the train only stopped once and this was for us to have tea made with hot water from the train's boiler. We arrived in Merville at midnight on the second day and laid down on the flag-stone road outside the railway station. Using our kit bags for pillows, we caught a precious few hours sleep. At 03.30 hours we were woken as the transport

'B' Flight of No. 87 Squadron take in the last of the summer sun at Debden in 1939. The pilots are (left to right) P/O Mackworth, P/O Cock, F/O Vose-Jeff, Sgt Thurgar, Sgt Peniket, P/O Joyce and Fritz the dog. Only Sgt Peniket, who was posted away in March 1940, escaped death or injury in the coming year. This snapshot was annotated with the names at the time. Note the pre-war issue flying overalls (Joyce).

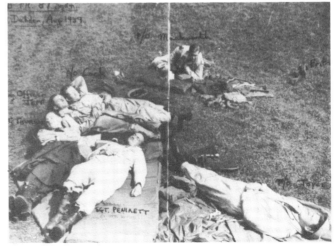

arrived. This consisted of four Crossley lorries which were more for the benefit of our equipment than ourselves. It was still dark when we arrived at the airfield and it was not until a few hours later, when dawn broke, that we were able to survey it. The airfield was literally a large field in which the Battle of Merville had been fought in World War I. On the far side of the airfield was a wooded area where our stores were kept. When walking through this wood I could clearly see the debris from the battles which had been fought 22 years before: empty shell cases, shattered trees and other relics laying half buried in the ground. On one side of the wood stood some intact concrete gun emplacements which had rusty chains embedded in their walls, we were told that the German gunners were chained to these during action. As I walked over the ground it felt very soft as the ground had still not settled from the shelling. A few weeks later, during October, the heavy rains turned Merville into a quagmire of mud and slush which caused the squadron's bus to get bogged down, one could easily visualise what the conditions in the trenches must have been.''

Throughout October there was no sign of the enemy, but the squadron remained busy flying over anti-aircraft batteries to assist in improving the gunner's recognition skills. On 6 October, Sergeant Witty was killed when he inexplicably crash landed Hurricane L1776. This was the squadrons first fatality of the war.

The occasional reconnaissance sortie by the Luftwaffe gave the pilots but fleeting glimpses of the adversary before they vanished into cloud. On 2 November, however, the squadron had their first opportunity for combat. Flight Lieutenant Vose-Jeff subsequently submitted the following report:

''The squadron was ordered to readiness, with 12 aircraft. At 10.45 hours, 'A' and 'B' Flights took off to intercept six enemy machines on reconnaissance. Two German aircraft flew directly over Merville and were fired on by British Bofors guns situated around the airfield until it was seen that they were being intercepted by the squadron. I saw what appeared to be sky writing (making vapour trails) but could not see any aircraft, I followed the sky writing for 20 minutes, climbing on until I saw the aircraft. It appeared to be doing a speed of about 180 mph. The rear underneath gunner opened fire with about 600 rounds, I held my fire until I got to 300 yards, opening fire from slightly underneath and behind until streams of black smoke came out of his engine. I followed him down and watched him put his wheels down to try and land in a field. On landing, the undercarriage collapsed but no damage was caused to the aircraft.''

Flight Lieutenant Vose-Jeff was later awarded the French 'Croix de Guerre avac Palme' by General Vuillemin for shooting down this, the first Luftwaffe aircraft to fall on French soil in World War 2. Pilot Officers Chris Mackworth, 'Dimmy' Joyce and 'Dennis' David attacked a

Malayan born Robert Vose-Jeff had been with the squadron since 1937 and was known as 'Social Type Jeff' because he wore the smartest uniform. Here he is presented with the Croix de Guerre avec Palme, by General Vuillemin.

second Heinkel He 111 which was last seen going down out of control over Belgium. Mackworth wrote to his wife, Jane, on 4 November.

''It was about 10 O'clock and we were puddling around our tent, or sitting outside, as it was a typical autumn day; pale blue sky and a thick haze over the ground, and very cold. Suddenly someone looked up and said there was a twin engine aeroplane over the aerodrome, so I rushed out to my 'Old Lady' and they started her up and I took off, and followed more or less the course I had seen the other machine taking. It never entered my head that it was anything but an English plane, so I thought I had got a free trip. I climbed up and it got very cold so I turned on my oxygen. Above the mist it was heavenly, you could hardly see the ground because of it, but high up there wasn't a cloud or a bump and the sun was lovely, so I pulled the cockpit hood shut and settled down. At 15,000 feet I stopped climbing and looked about. I saw another Hurricane following me, but took no notice of him and continued my search. Suddenly I looked down to my left, and about 2,000 feet below I saw a grey aeroplane flying in the opposite direction to me.

'Ah', said I, 'A Blenheim', so I took a look and flew down above it, and then saw two large white crosses on it. I'll always remember that moment. I knew at last that it was a real German quite close to me and that I should have to attack it. It all seemed so funny that we were alone up there, just us, and that we should have to fight up there all by ourselves. It looked such an ordinary aeroplane like I have seen so many times, and yet the crosses on it's wings stood out very strongly and sort of provoked me. It seemed so easy to just run away and pretend I hadn't seen him, and everyone would be happy. Still that wouldn't be a very good thing, so I turned round and got down on his tail. Two long plumes of smoke came out from the engines, and then I knew that they had seen me and were going flat out to escape. I also knew the battle was on. I got right down in the cockpit, set the sights and waited. Slowly he came nearer, it was such a queer feeling just waiting. Then I saw little blue things flying past close to me on my left and I knew that he was shooting. I pressed my tit and the old guns started. I waited for it to roll over or catch fire, but nothing happened. We got closer and both went on firing, then there was a cloud of smoke and oil and petrol from my machine so I deduced I was 'hors de combat'. I broke away and looked round and thought my Hurri was going to catch fire, but it didn't so I came down to an aerodrome and landed. It had eight bullet holes in the wings and tanks. That is my first encounter with brother Bosch. 'Dimmy' Joyce, who was behind me, attacked the enemy aircraft and it was forced to land in Belgium.''

Pilot Officer Dennis David was also involved in this combat and received bullets in his wing tips. The other incident of this day was when Pilot Officer St John's Hurricane

Pre-war glamour. The squadron's Gladiators neatly lined up at Debden in 1938, in the pre-war silver finish with the elaborate squadron markings on fuselage and across the wing tops (Peckett).

Left: Dunn's Hurricane after landing at Kutrijk on November 10, 1939. See also the picture on page 9.

Below: Johnny Dewar shakes the hand of His Majesty The King at Lille on December 6, 1939. In the background is F/Lt Colmore.

was mistaken for a German fighter over Dunkerque. His aircraft was hit by anti-aircraft fire and was written off on landing at Merville.

Mackworth's Heinkel landed in Belgium but it was not allowed to be inspected due to the country's nutrality. Vose-Jeff's Heinkel, on the other hand, landed in France and soon made news in the national daily's on English breakfast tables.

During the next few days a replacement Hurricane arrived for Pilot Officer St John and the squadron was ordered to move to Seclin, near Lille. On 6 November, Pilot Officer 'Roddy' Rayner incurred the displeasure of a French pilot when he attacked and forced down a Potez bomber, fortunately without injury to the crew.

All of the pilots with the squadron at this early stage of the war were very experienced peace-time flyers over Britain and had amassed many hours on Hurricanes. Navigation had rarely proved much of a problem to them over Britain, where they knew their landmarks and could easily locate their airfields. But in France, things were not so straight forward. In the early months of their deployment, many pilots became lost over the endless patchwork of fields and tiny villages. This resulted in many a forced landing, sometimes with disastrous consequences.

On 10 November 1939, Pilot Officer Dunn chased an enemy aircraft into Belgium and, finding himself lost and short of fuel, landed Hurricane L1619 at Kutrijk. Dunn was interned by the neutral Belgium authorities.

Four days later, Squadron Leader Coope, with Flying Officers 'Dicky' Glyde and 'Dimmy' Joyce, took off on an unsuccessful interception of a reconnaissance flight which was heading towards Boulogne. On their return, in thick cloud, they missed the airfield at Seclin and penetrated deep into Belgium airspace. After unsuccessfully trying to fix their position, Squadron Leader Coope lead the flight northwest until they hit the coast at Ostend. Here, the anti aircraft gunners were sufficiently angered by the intrusion to fire a barrage. Following the coast towards the French border, Coope's engine finally stopped due to lack of fuel and he was forced to make a landing on the beach at La Panne. Flying Officer 'Dicky' Glyde followed him down and landed on the beach close to his commander, only to be reminded that he was still in Belgium! Escape was now out of the quesiton, for both machines were stuck fast in the soft sand. Flying Officer 'Dimmy' Joyce carried on to land at Dunkirk and spread the news to the squadron.

Squadron Leader Coope was a bizzare character, as 'Dimmy' Joyce recalls, for he had been the Air Attache in Warsaw for some time and spoke fluent German and Polish. Both he and Glyde were duly interned and sent to Antwerp, where they were reunited with Pilot Officer Dunn. After a

few days under arrest, all three were allowed out on parole and began to make themselves at home in the city. Whilst sitting at a Cafe, a lady joined the three pilots and introduced herself as a British agent. Apparently knowing full well their predicament, she described the proposed escape method. The pilots were to wait outside their fort at midnight one week from then and all would be arranged. After accustoming their guards to the practice of taking late night runs around the fort, they simply disappeared and were delivered to the French border by the agent. All three were safely back at their airfield on 27 November and then proceeded back to England for debriefing.

The remainder of November passed without undue incident. Pilot Officer Smith landed at Dollai after his throttle stuck, Squadron Leader Hill assumed command of the Squadron from Coope, Flying Officer Campbell attacked an aircraft over Dunkerque and Sergeant 'Dinky' Howell turned his Hurricane on its nose at Le Touquet. Two new pilots joined the squadron, Pilot Officers Saunders and Beamont.

The squadron were honoured with a visit from the King, on 6 December. His visit lasted just 40 minutes, but in that time he, the Duke of Gloucester and Viscount Gort inspected the men and machines of both No 87 and No 85 Squadrons.

On 9 December, Sergeant 'Dinky' Howell was given the task of collecting a Hurricane from Glisy airfield, near Amiens:

''A new Hurricane was awaiting collection at Glisy and it fell to the new boy to pick it up. No spare map seemed to be available and the van driver who ran me to Glisy loaned me a scruffy road map. On arrival at Glisy in the afternoon I discovered the Hurricane to be of the latest mark, with a variable pitch, three bladed airscrew. I had never seen one before, but a fitter assured me that I would find a vast improvement in the take off performance. Having completely checked the aircraft and signed acceptance papers etc, I was ready to go. The aircraft, of course, had no squadron markings of any sort and no radio equipment, so when in the air I was going to be very lonely. By the time I buzzed off it was late afternoon, but my goodness the fitter was right. With the airscrew set to fine pitch for take off the aeroplane fairly screamed off the ground. So elated was I indeed, I couldn't resist beating the airfield up prior to setting course for Seclin (Lille). As I neared the industrial trio towns of Lille, Roubaix and Tourcoing, the visibility was very poor and daylight rapidly fading. I followed what I thought to be the road out to Seclin from Lille at about 500 feet with visibility by this time just vertically down through the industrial haze. But, unfortunately for me, someone had moved the airfield!

After some rapid investigation of other roads it was now apparent that I must force land the aircraft or bale out. What a dreadful loss of the new aeroplane to desert it, so I stuck to it and put it down in a small field (to avoid cattle in a larger field which had been a first selection). My approach into the small field was fraught with danger as H/T cables appeared in the gloom just as I was about to hold off, fully flapped and wheels down! I burst the throttle just enough to hold my nose down above the H/T cables, but not enough to prevent a very heavy landing. The undercart collapsed, the aircraft dropped onto the airscrew and after some peculiar gyrations in the muddy field I finally came to rest. Lucky old me again! Second forced landing and still in one piece, but not the aeroplane this time.. A quick inspection revealed, of course, the damaged undercart and prop blades all shortened by at least a foot or so. It did not look beyond repair and I had visions of it being repaired in the squadron workshop.

"I had only been on the ground for a very short time when out of the gloom appeared a young man, out of breath having run rapidly over a fair distance. He looked at me, then at the aircraft, and said in French "Royal Air Force?" I said "yes", to which he immediately requested me to follow him straight away with great urgency. I collected my maps and parachute and we ran to a point where he directed me to hurry through a little copse to the French frontier! He wished me God's Speed and informed me that I was in Belgium and that the noises I could hear in the distance would be Belgian police who intended to intern me.

"At the frontier, the French guards cheered me on and pulled me over the fence. There I waited for the friendly Belgian police to arrive. They, of course, said that I really must return to Belgium to discuss internment etc. and I naturally said that I preferred the climate in France. To cut this long story short, the Station Commander, Wing Commander Atcherly, was very angry with me as he was not aware that the aeroplane was in the wrong country and arrived in the very early hours of the following morning with quite a lot of salvage gear. However, the Belgian Air Force had a Hurricane squadron and I think they eventually purchased the aeroplane for their squadron."

The terrible weather conditions which now clamped Europe in frost and snow put a halt to almost all operations by No 87 Squadron. Excitement was created when the Prime Minister, the Right Honourable Neville Chamberlain, paid the squadron a visit. Another selection of pilots were presented, but no less than eighty men took the opportunity to go to Lens to see 'Me and My Girl' starring Lupino Lane and Teddie St Dennis. Following the show many toured the cafes of Lens in search of wine and 'other pleasures which France is famous for'.

This was all very well for the officers but, as Reg Guppy recalls, the Erk's lot was not altogether a happy one.

"As I look back over the years to those early days of the

The King's inspection of sister squadron, No 85 shows well the finish of a Hurricane in late 1939. Note on VY-X, the squadron commander's emblem below the cockpit canopy, and the gas detection patch on the wingtip. Note camouflaged Gladiators opposite.

war in France, the first thing I recall is how very different it was to those balmy days of peace time.

"How very different were our living conditions and work routine. We now had to be up well before dawn for 'dawn readiness'. The aircraft guard, made up of our own squadron members, would have to give those of us who had to be up on the airfield and have the kites ready for take off before dawn, an early call. As the guard had to find those of us so detailed in the dark, the nett result was that all the squadron got an early call!

"Perhaps the most important erk to get a call was the duty cook. As the rest of us got ready by torchlight (for those lucky enough to have one), we would gather at the most convenient place, the cookhouse trailer, where hopefully the

'Dinky' Howell as a sergeant in France, 1939 (Howell).

Below: On January 11, 1940, the Squadron received a visit from the RAF's official photographers. Beamont's groundcrew proudly display a cross from Vose-Jeff's Heinkel.

Above: A fine view of a Hurricane I at 87 Squadron in the pre-war colours with underside silver and with wing undersides black and white with serials in contrast. This is in August 1939, at Debden. Airman Reg Guppy is on the nose of Hurricane L1619. This aircraft later forced landed in Belgium on November 10, 1939, flown by P/O Dunn (Guppy).

cook would have a dixy of char mashed. There were usually a few hard tack biscuits around, hard as hell and tasteless, some even tasted of candles as they were wrapped in waxed paper.

''The early morning crews usually consisted of about three crews each from 'A' and 'B' Flights. A crew was a mechanic and rigger and the team was made up with a few armourers and wireless operators, and a couple of odd bods like drivers and mates. A few NCOs would make up the party, who would set off either on foot or transport, depending on the distance to the kites.

''On arrival at the dispersal, the guard would make their exit and we would gather at the flight office which might only be a tent or a lorry, very occasionally a building. We would be briefed as to which kites would be on first take off etc. Although we had our own regular kites, for dawn readiness it was possible to have any of the flights' kites to look after.

''The first thing was to get the starter accumulators to the readiness kites. These starter accumulators were housed in two-wheeled trolleys with metal handles for pulling them along. They also had a heavy duty cable and pin plug which fitted a socket on the kite and the trolley was fitted with a 'press to start' switch. The whole thing weighed a couple of hundredweight.

Cockpit covers and engine covers were removed and wing picket ropes released. Wheel chocks checked, a quick look under the engine to see if any leaks had developed overnight and then it was into the cockpit, first removing the control's locking device and stowing it away in the cockpit; meanwhile the rigger would stand by the starter acc. to be ready for start up. A check to see that it was all clear to start the engine and then start-up.

''Most mechs had the feel of the Merlin engines and had no difficulty starting them up in quick time.

''During warm up the recognised procedure was always carried out. Having checked all that had to be checked the engine was stopped and, if necessary, the petrol tank was topped up.

''During this time the other trades would be doing their own check. All was now ready for the pilots to take over. By now dawn would be just breaking and it would be light enough to see to take off. If it was to be a patrol, the first section of two or perhaps more would get airborne.

''This was the time for us to get the four gallon tins of petrol from the nearest petrol dump over to where the kites were parked. In the early days in France, kites were refuelled by hand using petrol funnels in which a chamois leather was placed to catch the water in the tins.

''During the months that we were in France we were to experience all types of weather, from sunny and warm to the other extreme of ice and snow, but the conditions that I remember the best were the mud and water-logged airfields. Here not only was refuelling a problem, but every aspect of aircraft handling was one hard slog, it was common to have to literally lift the aircraft up on the backs of the erks underneath the wings to get the kites even to taxi in the mud. It was a common sight to see kites taking off more like speed-boats than aircraft and many a kite has flipped over on its back coming into land on the water-logged airfields. I am quite satisfied that no other fighter aircraft before or since would have put up with the treatment that the Hurricane endured in France in 1939 and 1940.

With the arrival of the remainder of the flight after they had breakfasted, the dawn mob would depart for their breakfast. As almost all that we ate came out of tins, and as

Pilots who flew operational flights with 87 Squadron, September 1939 to December 1941

F/Lt Colmore	Sgt Thurgar	P/O Watson	Sgt Penikett	Sgt Want	P/O Shimmons	Sgt Gallus
Sgt Witty	F/Lt Vose-Jeff	P/O Mitchell	Sgt Culverwell	Sgt Stirling	Sgt Hughes	P/O Malarowski
Sgt Cowley	P/O Dunn	P/O Beamont	F/Sgt Badger	P/O Malengreau	W/Cdr Beamish	P/O Grantham
F/O Campbell	P/O David	P/O Jay	Sgt Walton	Sgt Wood	Sgt Castle	Sgt Horsham
P/O St. John	P/O Cock	P/O Darwin	Sgt Wakeling	Sgt Thom	Sgt Longbridge	Sgt F. C. Robinson
P/O Rayner	P/O Mackworth	F/Lt Robinson	Sgt Thorogood	Sgt Milburn	P/O Denville	Sgt H. J. Robinson
P/O Glyde	P/O Edwards	No record for	S/Ldr Lovell-Gregg	P/O Musgrove	Sgt Rogerson	Sgt Henry
S/Ldr Coope	Sgt Howell	April 1940	P/O Mclure	F/Lt Fordham	Sgt Harding	Sgt Banks
P/O Tait	S/Ldr Traill	F/O Stickland	P/O Roscoe	F/Lt Denison	P/O Jewell	Sgt Miller
F/O Smith	S/Ldr Dewar	F/O Ward	P/O Carver	F/O Smallwood	Sgt Chivers	Sgt Rogers
Sgt Nowell	S/Ldr Hill	P/O Comely	F/O Laycock	F/O Forsyth	Sgt Gibbs	Sgt Thompson
P/O Joyce	P/O Saunders	F/Lt Gleed	P/O De Spirlet	F/O Laycock	Sgt Beda	

This list does not include ferry pilots who flew with the Squadron during the Battle of France and did not return from combat.

Just before war was declared somebody took this atmospheric photograph of 'B' Flight on stand-by at Debden. A Hurricane is dispersed at left and the ground crew in the background are gathering up the stores and fittings while the pilots await the call to action.

the variety of tins was limited, the meals were repetative. Bully beef and tinned stew being the menu most often seen. The meals were usually taken at trestle tables and wooden forms located somewhere near the cookhouse trailer. All the erks carried and used their own mug and eating irons and had the grub dished up in either a mess tin or on an enamel plate, which was washed in the tub of hot water provided. This, after several dozen plates had been washed in it, was both cold and greasy.

"On return to the airfield after breakfast, the daily inspection of the kites would begin. All the erks would be present except the guard who would have the morning off. Depending on the state of readiness, time had to be found for each kite to have it's daily inspection, which formed part of a laid down procedure, from between flights, and depending on hours flown by regular stages right up to major overhaul, but not many kites lasted that long.

"The mechanic and his mate the rigger would take off the various panels to both the engine and the airframe and inspect all the things as laid down and at the same time keep an eye open for anything else that might be amiss. The other trades would appear also and do their inspections, the armourer being the next major contributor to the mayhem. After everything was found to be in order and all adjustments had been made, all the panels were replaced and the engine tested and run-up on the ground to full throttle, after which all trades had to sign the form 700. This was also signed by the NCOs and lastly by the pilot before take off. It might be necessary for a mech and rigger to 'daily inspection' more than one kite if other crews were away. The routine of flying and refuelling went on as long as those above deemed it necessary. There was no nine to five routine and no demarcation disputes, you just got on with it.

"As the Hurricane had not been in the service very long before the outbreak of the war, it still had a lot of teething troubles to be sorted out. In 1939, for example, the S/U carburettors, the coolant pumps, the air compressors, the oleo legs, the coolant tanks, problems with overheating and several problems with keeping the starter accs. charged sufficiently to get the engines started. The biggest problems of all were undoubtedly the sparking plugs and the internal coolant leaks, both of which kept the maintenance flight busy.

At dusk or shortly after we would get 'released' for the day and after bedding the kites down the guard would take over.

"On our return to our sleeping quarters not too many creature comforts were to be found. About the only one supplied was a canvas paliasse which was a mattress cover into which straw was stuffed through a slot in the side. Care had to be taken to get only the right amount of straw in and evenly spread, otherwise it was like sleeping on an ant hill! Lights were also virtually non-existent but torches were still able to be purchased if a town was near at hand. As far as accommodation was concerned, it varied with the location, from a corn silo, a lorry garage, several farm outbuildings, aircraft hangars (without doors), the odd house and tents.

I suppose the best remembered was the corn silo at Merville. This was a gaunt concrete building situated by a canal. It was open at one end on the ground floor where the lorries entered; on the first floor there was a balcony around three sides with a large opening to the ground floor. On the top floor was where all the troops lived, with those that could not squash in having to occupy the balcony on the first floor. It was dodgy after dark, as it was quite easy to fall down to the ground floor over the balcony. There was also a

Above: Vose-Jeff (2nd right) and Dennis David (right) at Lille. Note the gaiters!

Left: More publicity. First time flight in a Hurricane as reported in the comic 'Modern Boy' on May 13, 1939. Though anonymous it was in fact, written by Pilot Officer Chris Mackworth of 87 Squadron.

sack chute from the top floor, which was a popular way down.

"A great deal of ingenuity was given to the provision of beds to prevent having to sleep on the concrete floor. The plentiful supply of petrol boxes helped a great deal and these were adapted, not only into beds, but lockers and even chairs and tables. The petrol tins themselves, although a disaster for holding petrol as they all leaked after the rough handling they got from Blighty to France, were a boon as wash basins when cut down. It was not unknown to have a bath with two cut down tins and a foot placed in each. A supply of hot water would have made it more pleasureable! Everytime we moved, which was often, all the comforts had to be ditched, except the pallias which was emptied, in the hope that a supply of straw would be forthcoming at the next location.

"In retrospect I think of all the useless issue kit that we had to carry with us in the limited transport, which could have been swapped for items much more practical.

"The early days of our stay in France were not at all doom and gloom as we had lots to laugh at, especially as we were young and in a foreign land and had lots to learn. It was great to be able to get out of camp and partake of the local food and drink at the nearest village. If you could find a lady to do the dhoby, you had really arrived!

"For those who have called and regard the early days of the war in France as the Phoney War, all I can say is that a lot of us who took part grew from boys into men in a short space of time.''

Christmas Day was spent in the traditional manner when the officer's invited the sergeant's mess to drink the Loyal Toast. Both officers and NCOs then served Christmas dinner to the ground crews. As a finale to the celebrations, the officers staged a show which came to an abrupt end when Australian, Johnny Cock, took to the stage. Quite what part of his repertoir of Aussi humour was given has gone unrecorded, but it must have been bad as it prompted the ground crews to launch a barrage of oranges at Johnny Cock, a waste as they were part of their Christmas treat!

The New Year saw little change and was opened in a spectacular manner on 3 January by 'Dimmy' Joyce, accidentally retracting the undercarriage of Hurricane N2353 on the landing run. He had apparently intended to put the flaps up but, what ever the cause, the aircraft was considerably damaged as it slid along on its belly.

On 14 January, a most disturbing piece of news was received. All leave was cancelled as of 13.00 hours, due to the possible invasion of Belgium and Holland. As if stirred by this, the Commanding Officer gathered his pilots together to discuss tactics and methods of attack. The snow and frost converted the landing ground into a concrete hard, bumpy field. This gave rise to the possibility of damage being caused to tail wheels and shock absorbers and consequently flying was kept to a minimum. Even so, Sergeant Thurgar was flying Hurricane L1613 on 12 February, when visibility deteriorated during his flight over Nantes to such an extent that he was forced down and died in the resulting crash.

The whole squadron moved back to Le Touquet on 20 February, to carry out training exercises. One of these involved a borrowed drogue, towed behind an aircraft, for the squadron to fire at. All went well until the drogue came detached and fell into the sea. Ground targets were then selected and Bofors and Bren gun positions on Stella Plage

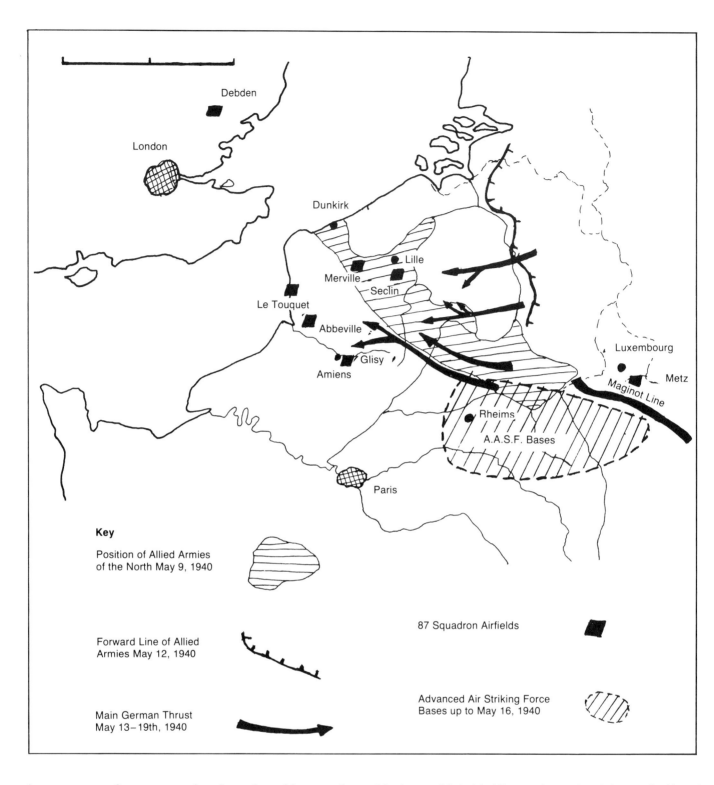

Key

Position of Allied Armies
of the North May 9, 1940

Forward Line of Allied
Armies May 12, 1940

Main German Thrust
May 13–19th, 1940

87 Squadron Airfields

Advanced Air Striking Force
Bases up to May 16, 1940

became targets for more practice. Several notable generals watched the spectacle and suggested that it be repeated daily for the benefit of the troops.

The squadron returned to Seclin, on 6 March, and detachments were sent to Merville for continued air-to-ground firing practice. Two pilots, Flight Lieutenant Robinson, the newly arrived 'A' Flight commander and Pilot Officer Jay, both made forced landings whilst returning from this. Rumours of German invasion were building and ground crews were set to work digging trenches and carrying out anti-gas routines.

The appallingly cold winter which was described in the *Paris Soir* as "as unbearable as Nazi-ism" was beginning to come to an end and the thaw brought back the floods and mud baths of the autumn. During April, the squadron moved first to Glisy and then to Senon, near Metz, but conditions were the same all over northern France. Operations consisted of escort missions to No 2 Squadron Lysanders which were engaged on photographic sorties over the

Maginot and Seigfried lines. The mud took its usual toll on 6 May, when Flight Lieutenant Robinson and Flying Officer Tait overturned a Master. Later that day newly arrived Squadron Leader Dewar also overturned a Hurricane.

Pilot Officer Dunn and Sergeant Nowell were on patrol over the Maginot Line on 9 May. At 22,000 feet they sighted a twin finned aircraft which they identified as a Dornier Do 215. Nowell immediately closed in to a range of 200 yards and, keeping his finger on the gun button, he fired all his ammunition in a continuous burst of 12 to 14 seconds. Dunn then made three attacks before the Dornier escaped into clouds with pieces falling away. Nowell returned to land at Seclin, but Dunn ran into trouble when his fuel ran out and forced him land once more in a field.

87 Squadron had been sent to France as part of No 60 Wing, the air component of the British Expeditionary Force. In addition to providing air support for the BEF, No 60 Wing was to assist the Armee de L'Air in the defence of France, should the country be invaded by Germany.

12

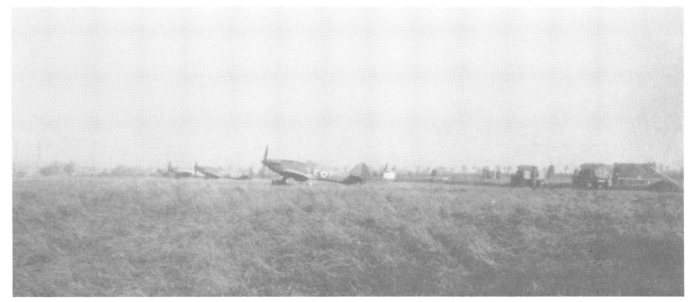

A poor quality snapshot shows 87 Squadron dispersed on the First World War battlefield of Merville soon after their arrival in France in 1939.

2. Battle of France

The Armee de L'Air, had become the victim of political uncertainty in the 1920s and 30s when each successive government appointed new Air Ministers, each of whom had different opinions as to how any air forces should be employed. This effectivly prevented the creation of an

Garry Nowell at Merville. He became the top scorer of the Battle of France before being shot down three times in a week and finally shot in the foot by a French soldier which put him in hospital for eighteen months.

efficient air defence for France. The front line fighter power available to the French in May 1940 was:

8 Groups of Bloch fighters (200 machines)
11 Groups of Morane fighters (275 machines)
1 Group of Dewoitine fighters (25 machines)
4 Groups of Curtiss Hawk fighters (100 machines)

To this force was added a further 11 groups of Polish and Czechoslovakian origin (275 machines) and the RAF contribution of two Gladiator squadrons and four Hurricane squadrons. With the exception of the RAF's Hurricanes, these aircraft could easily be outfought by the Messerschmitt Bf 109 with which the Luftwaffe fighter units were equipped. Although figures are in some confusion as to the total number of aircraft available to the Luftwaffe in May 1940, they are generally accepted to be in the order of 3,800 front line machines, 860 of which were Me 109s.

"Soldiers of the West Front! The battle which is beginning today will decide the fate of German nation for the next thousand years." Adolf Hitler, 10 May 1940.

Early in the morning of 10 May, the threats and rumours of German invasion became reality as 'Operation Gelb' was launched. Holland, Belgium and Luxemburg were simultaneously invaded by overwhelming numbers of troops, to which the Anglo-French response was a counter invsion of Belgium and Holland under the Dyle Plan. General Gamelin, the Allied Commander-in-Chief, issued his order of the day and announced:

"Germany has engaged in a war to the death against us, have courage, energy, confidence."

As Europe was launched into all-out war, the personnel of No 87 Squadron at Metz were awakened by the noise of a tremendous anti-aircraft barrage and the drone of aero engines vibrating the air. A deep, thudding sound which the squadron had not heard before began to rent the air. Bombs were exploding! Four of the squadron's pilots were in the air by 05.30 hours, in pursuit of some 60 enemy aircraft.

Flight Lieutenant Vose-Jeff attacked a formation of 12 Dorniers and three Me 110s bombing Thionville. After several attacks on a Dornier at the rear of the formation the enemy "wobbled badly" just as his Hurricane was hit by return fire. Glycol from the Hurricane's cooling system

Reg Guppy the fitter seen on duty at Merville.

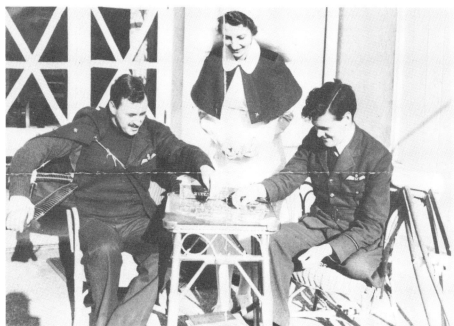

'Dimmy' Joyce had his leg amputated after his crash on May 14th. Here he recovers at the Palace Hotel, Torquay, in October (Joyce).

flooded into the cockpit, temporarily blinding Vose-Jeff, who made a forced landing at Doncourt. A Dornier Do 17, the crew of which was captured, crashed at Boulanges at this time and was believed to have been the aircraft he had attacked.

Pilot Officer Edwards attacked a Heinkel He 111 flying at 12,000 feet over Luxemburg but, after a four second burst, he was forced to break off his attack. Fourteen Dornier Do 17s were then sighted and Edwards made an attack on the rearmost machine. After a three or four second burst the Dornier went down and crashed, leaving the remainder of the formation heading east, for Germany.

Roughly an hour later, at 06.12 hours, Sergeant Nowell was pursuing some aircraft into Luxemburg and later reported:

"I saw two aircraft, which I took to be Lysanders, but coming below them I saw black crosses and realised that they were Henschel Hs 126s. I attacked, but the aircraft at which I was aiming turned steeply. I followed and blacked out through the 'G' forces, when I came round I saw an aircraft almost immediately in front of me. I fired and saw strikes on the aircraft which dived towards the ground and blew up. The second Henschel was still turning above when I attacked it in the same way and shot it down. On returning to base I managed to arrange confirmation of both victories with the help of Pilot Officer David. On our next patrol we flew over the area of this combat and saw two large holes, surrounded by wreckage."

Shortly after midday, nine Dornier Do 17s attempted to bomb the airfield at Metz, but none of the 20 bombs found their target. A salvo of five bombs fell in a corner of a nearby forest, but failed to silence a cuckoo which kept up its happy song throughout the raid.

Pilot Officers Saunders and Dennis David attacked six Dornier Do 17s at 12.20 hours, some five miles south of Thionville, flying at 10,000 feet. Both pilots made stern attacks and saw parts falling away from one machine and another diving with smoke streaming from it. Saunders pressed home his attack against concentrated return fire and fired a long burst into one bomber before the Hurricane's radiator was hit and glycol streamed into the cockpit, temporarily blinding the pilot. Despite the damage to his aircraft, Saunders returned safely to Metz, to which Dennis David had just returned and immediately taken off again. David was then joined by Sergeant Garry Nowell and

together they climbed above cloud to find six Dornier Do 17s that had bombed the town of Senon. After making a stern attack, David saw his target catch fire and fall away in flames to crash 10 miles south east of Thionville. Nowell also saw "his" Dornier go down in flames before turning his attention to a second bomber. Once again, the return fire was accurate and the radiator and engine of Nowell's Hurricane was hit. With fuel and glycol vapours stinging his eyes, Nowell brought the damaged Hurricane back to Metz, where the engine seized on approach to land. Negotiating trees and a row of parked Hurricanes, Nowell landed and brought the machine safely to a halt.

Later that afternoon, at 14.50 hours, Pilot Officer Campbell was one of six pilots who attacked four Dorniers over Meziers. Campbell claimed that one went down with both engines stopped and he then caused smoke to pour from two more bombers, but none were seen to crash. The final action of the day occured at 18.55 hours, when Pilot Officer Edwards attacked a Dornier over Lille. After his first attack, the Dornier's starboard engine caught fire and the bomber dived to ground level where Edwards continued his attacks until they were 20 miles into Belgium and he was forced to break off the chase and return to base with two bullet holes in his Hurricane.

On the second day of the Battle of France, 11 May, Pilot Officer Mitchell brought down one of 60 Junkers Ju 87s, bombing Brussels, into a forest south of the city. Mitchell, with Squadron Leader Dewar, then chased a Dornier Do 17, which had been deserted by its Me 109 escort and brought it down 15 miles north-east of Brussels.

12 May, brought continuous patrols, but no combats. The ground crews created a device which consisted of four Browning machine guns on a makeshift mounting which "looked grand and was very menacing".

The impetus of the German attack showed no sign of being halted on 13 May as the Panzer divisions, supported by air cover, helped to establish bridgeheads over the River Meuse at Sedan, Montherme and Dinant. In the air, a unit of French Dewoitine D-520 fighters were in action over the Meuse Front and claimed to have brought down four enemy aircraft without loss to themselves.

The pilots of No 87 Squadron were, as usual, in the thick of the fighting as Sergeant 'Dinky' Howell recalled.

"Having just returned from the very early morning patrol, pilots were told to remain in their aeroplanes as bombers were just forming up for an important target which was known to be heavily defended and needed all the fighter protection they could get. So off we went again, and this without the faintest idea where. Not only that, as I looked around at the other Hurricanes we had strangers with us and I found myself flying No 3 to the Flight Commander, F/Lt Campbell, with a stranger in the No 2 position.

"We had not been airborne very long when we were obviously spotted by a wing of 109s. They came from the sun, with altitude advantage and I never even saw them. Suddenly there was a shattering noise and the cockpit was full of burnt cordite and the aircraft adopted a 'no control situation'; then as I attempted to pull the aeroplane around into a very steep turn, another shattering explosion in the wing area and the aircraft pulled its nose into a peculiar stall position, followed by odd gyrations. To stay with the aircraft meant death, and perhaps the parachute was the answer. After a struggle with the hood I unfastened my safety straps and went rocketing out of the aircraft. I estimated that we were escorting at about 16,000 feet and by the time the aircraft and myself parted company I was at about 8,000 feet. As the 'chute opened it was obvious that it wasn't going to fully open. As it spilt air from one side I started to gyrate slowly and swing rather like a pendulum. When I got to the last 200 feet or so, it was obvious to me that I was falling too fast (although I had never made a parachute descent before); but I think the odd swing and spin took some of the shock off as I crunched into a freshly ploughed field. However the contact with terra firma was heavy enough to knock me out.

"I have no idea how long I was out, but on coming to, some peasant ladies were trying to release my parachute harness which was still dragging me across the field. We managed it together, but the men stood over me with what appeared to be sticks and attempted to converse with me in a strange tongue. It sounded very much like German to my untrained ears and then in the midst of this failure of both parties to understand, a voice in French suddenly said

Garry Nowell with wife Freda at Buckingham Palace, still walking with sticks after his recovery from the action described on page 18.

'Garry' Nowell, was christened Gareth Loefric Nowell and came from Cheshire. After moving to No 32 Squadron he was shot down for a third time over France, during the evacuation of Dunkirk on 23 May. After 18 months in hospital recovering from a bullet in his leg, he was posted to No 61 OTU as an instructor. Then followed postings to Nos 124, 610 and 616 Squadrons, he ended the war with 16 victories to his credit. Post-war, Garry went into the motor trade and now enjoys his retirement in Sussex, with his wife Freda and keeps himself busy restoring Morris Minor cars to show room condition.

'Dimmy' Joyce's life was changed by the events of 14 May 1940, when he was shot down over Belgium. After being freed from his crashed Hurricane, evacuated from France and losing a leg through gangrene, he eventually retired to Berkshire where he lives with his wife Joan.

A Hurricane, destroyed at Lille by the RAF during the retreat (Kochy via Trivett).

"English flyer." I replied in the affirmative and it was smiles all round and they carried me into a farmhouse on a sheep hurdle as they, like me, thought that I had seriously hurt my back.

"Whilst I enjoyed some hot coffee, rolls and jam, the kind farmers had 'phoned for a doctor. On his arrival he wasted no time in sliding me, still fixed to the hurdle, into his shooting brake and off we went, after my appropriate thank yous, etc, for all their help and kindness.

"The reason for them not understanding my schoolboy French or me the rather strange tongue, was that I had chosen to bale out over the Flemish speaking part of Belgium; and the urgency shown by the doctor was due to German patrols having been seen in the area.

"The doctor dropped me at the Brussels General Hospital and after a series of X-ray examinations discovered that I had no broken bones but some severe bruising and some abrasions on my hands and face. The hospital was overflowing with terribly wounded soldiers from the Belgian front, and how it brings home to you the stupidity of war when massed wounded soldiers are observed in a group for the first time. As a result of the overflow state I was transferred to a hospital in Ghent to recuperate for a few days and thereby hangs another strange tale.

"I met the Hurricane (Belgian) pilots who had been badly shot up on the ground trying to take off. Several were badly burned and others suffered cruel injuries. However, in the general chats we had about fighter aircraft, they said that in the early or middle part of December the previous year a stupid RAF pilot had lost his way and landed the latest mark of Hurricane in their beautiful country, and that it ended it's days flying with their squadron. Was my face red, and howls of laughter accompanied the admission that the said stupid pilot was yours truly! Although the day had seemed a lifetime, it was still only 13 May 1940.

"With the full knowledge that the Hun must be getting very close to Ghent, on the morning of the 15 May, I decided that the time had come for me to try to get back to my unit, although still in considerable pain and with a backbone structure like that of a bent pin. I soon found the attaché, or some senior official in Ghent, who stated that he would help me (albeit the roads and rail were still jammed with the BEF trying to move up) and would I spend another day and night with some of his friends who lived just out of town while he tried to organise some transport. The friends turned out to be rich flax merchants who had arranged a farewell party that very night for all the British contingent which included themselves, the local golf pro, doctor, government officials, etc. What a party. All the local wine cellars came with the various groups – all champagne I would think – it never stopped flowing. Oh! my head the next day, all of my other pains had been transferred to my head!

"The official finally regretted that I could not expect any help from him unless I wished to return to the UK by sea from the coast somewhere. Thanking him, but gently refusing his offer and bidding a fond farewell to all, I boldly struck out for Lille on foot, soon to be swept along on a tide of refugees, many of whom knew not where to terminate the journey. Although so many years have passed since those terrible days and I have worked and mixed with many fine German scientists and their families since, I have never really forgiven the Luftwaffe for machine-gunning miles and miles of helpless refugees on open roads, when it was so obvious that these were refugees to the eyes behind the gunsights. I know that they have often said that armed fighting troops were mixed in with the refugees, but may God still forgive them."

'Dinky' Howell was not the only pilot of No 87 Squadron who failed to return from the day's fighting, for the flight

'Kit' Mackworth and his wife Jane who were married only months before his death in the action recounted here (Jane Barrett).

commander of 'A' Flight, Flight Officer J. A. Campbell, and two ferry pilots were also lost. What became of the two ferry pilots is unknown for they had arrived the previous day with two replacement Hurricanes and had volunteered to stay with the squadron, even though neither had had any previous combat experience. One of these brave ferry pilots was presumably flying with 'Dinky' Howell as 'Number 2' to Campbell and was seen to go down with his machine, but the other simply went missing. Such was the state of confusion that the names of these two have gone unrecorded, save for a memory that one was perhaps a 'Sergeant Grew'. Campbell was last seen over Brussels and fell victim to the same Me 109s that claimed Howell and at least one of the ferry pilots. On the 'plus' side for the squadron, Flight Lieutenant 'Widge' Gleed claimed to have brought down an Me 109, whilst the Australian, Johnny Cock, brought down an He 111 at Armentiers. This Heinkel crashed in a field where, some 30 minutes later, the bomb load exploded and killed 36 bystanders.

On 14 May, an almost suicidal attempt to destroy pontoon bridges across the River Meuse at Sedan was made by 150 obsolete bombers such as Fairy Battles and Amiot 143s. After the loss of 50 aircraft, the bridges remained intact and Guderian's 1st Panzer Division continued to cross.

The pilots of No 87 Squadron once more suffered at the hands of the Luftwaffe, with two more pilots being killed and another terribly injured. Pilot Officer T. J. Edwards was last seen going down in flames over Belgium, whilst Chris Mackworth set off alone and single handedly attacked seven enemy aircraft. Although none of his fellow pilots were able to bear witness to this flight, Lieutenant E. R. Stanford of No 143 Field Ambulance, Royal Army Medical Corps, was determined that it would not pass untold and that Mackworth's death would not go unrecorded. Accordingly, he wrote to Pilot Officer Mackworth's father, Major Mackworth, on 2 June

Dear Major,

On the advance into Belgium we established an MDS at Bruyelles, near Tournai, map reference 948265. One of our companies established an advanced dressing station at Mainvault, near Ath. 14 May.

It was this company at Mainvault that picked up and sent to us a Pilot Officer of the RAF. This officer was dead on arrival at Bruyelles and it was stated that he was thought to be a German – perhaps because he came down by parachute.

The telegram received by Mrs Mackworth bringing the tragic news of her husband's death (Jane Barrett).

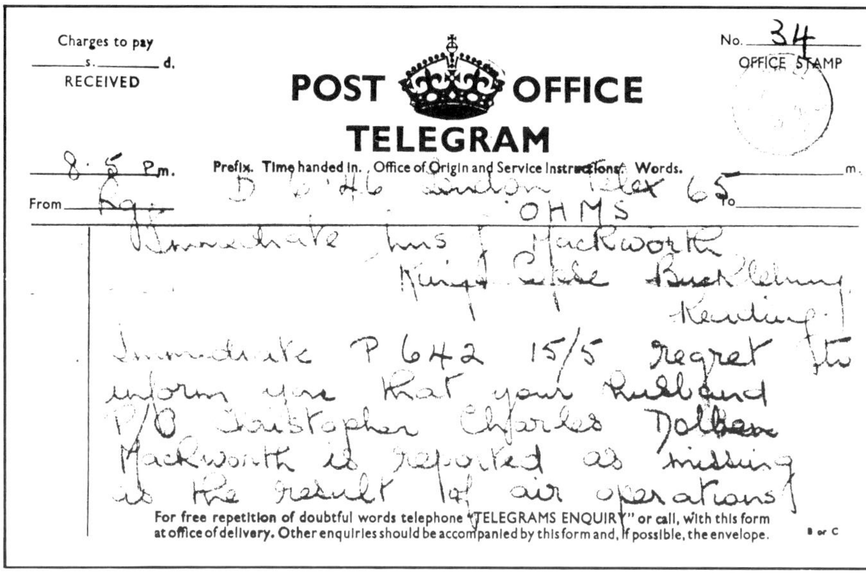

Charges to pay
s. d.
RECEIVED

No. 34
OFFICE STAMP

POST OFFICE
TELEGRAM

8.5 Pm.
Prefix. Time handed in. Office of Origin and Service Instructions. Words.
From Hq.
D 6'46 London Telex 65
OHMS

Immediate Mrs J Mackworth
Kings Coffee Bucklebury
Reading

Immediate P642 15/5 regret to inform you that your husband P/O Christopher Charles Dolben Mackworth is reported as missing as the result of air operations

For free repetition of doubtful words telephone "TELEGRAMS ENQUIRY" or call, with this form at office of delivery. Other enquiries should be accompanied by this form and, if possible, the envelope.
B or C

Below: In Spring 1940, Chris Mackworth married, but on May 14 1940, he was killed in action near Brussels. His widow, Jane, later re-married and in October, 1987, she made a journey to Belgium to visit Chris' grave (Jane Barrett).

Parts of his parachute were still attached to him, there were no identification marks on the clothing or body – only by his uniform we knew that he was a Pilot Officer RAF.

I buried him myself in the cemetery at Bruyelles – the Curate said the burial service. As there was no identity he was buried as an unknown Pilot Officer and the grave is marked with a cross (wood) and particulars in a beer bottle placed on the grave. This Officer was wearing a silver locket round his neck, inside the locket was a photograph of a lady – under the photograph was fair hair.

He is buried next to one other British soldier. 2982520 Pte Adams, Henry. Belgian women came afterwards and the two graves were piled high with lovely flowers.

Then we continued our advance up to Brussels. Next day we caught up with our Company and apparently the Belgian Police had reached the parachute first and taken off disc papers etc. These were handed to me and identity was established from disc with name in ink – 40728 Pilot Officer Mackworth. RAF.

There were a dozen letters from Mrs Mackworth, a pipe, cigarette case and various other odds and ends.

I sent an account of his death and the locket and letters to Mrs Mackworth.

Seven German planes came and machined gunned our ADS in the village and Mackworth took on the seven of them single handed – but odds were too many and he was shot down.

A burial certificate and all the other things were sent to Officer i/c Effects Branch, No 2 Echelon, Margate.

I fear that all letters have been lost as everything seems to have gone astray so hence my letter of yesterday.

These are the facts at my disposal and I shall be pleased to help any time you wish anything further.

Will you convey me deepest sympathy to Mrs Mackworth, for her husband was a brave man.

I am, Sir,
Yours sincerely,
E. R. Stanford.
Lieut RAMC 143 Field Ambulance."

One of the last to see Mackworth alive was Flying Officer 'Dimmy' Joyce, who had been due to fly the patrol with him.

"At about 7 pm on 14 May 1940, Chris Mackworth and I were 'at readiness' in our cockpits at Lille-Marc when we were ordered to investigate enemy activity over Louvain, (east of Brussels) Chris was having trouble starting his engine so I went off alone on an easterly heading.

"At 13,000 ft south of Brussels, I sighted a large formation of Messerschmitt Me 110s and having the advantage of the evening sun behind me I opened to maximum boost to get closer. Before getting within range I was spotted and an aircraft peeled off from the leading group in my direction. In reflex action I turned head on to meet him and managed to get a good burst of fire dead on his nose before it was necessary to thrust smartly forward on the control column to avoid a head-on collision. He flashed past just over my canopy, too close for comfort! He did not seem to fire his front 20 mm cannons. Turning sharply to see what he was doing, I saw him in a downward spiral, so I renewed the chase of the main formation and when in range opened fire on the aircraft on the extreme left. As there were a lot of tracers coming from the air-gunner in the aircraft at the rear section, I turned starboard to give him a short burst which seemed to silence him. I had just re-opened fire on the left-hand aircraft when there was a savage thump in my left leg, which went numb and looking down I saw that blood was spurting out below the knee.

"The next memory is of the aircraft plunging earthwards in a vertical dive. As the elevator controls seemed sloppy and ineffective I undid the straps to bale out, but could not move from the seat because the leg was seized at right angles on the rudder bar and there was something amiss with my left arm. In utter resignation I made another desperate attempt to get the aircraft out of the dive and eventually there was sufficient response from the elevators to level the aircraft at a low altitude. The engine was dead and when a tree-covered ridge appeared ahead I was unable to get adequate response from the controls to lift the aircraft over it. I recall nothing of the impact with the trees and only remember lying on the ground with bits of Hurricane and the setting sun shimmering through the trees.

"Not being sure whether I was in hostile territory, I was relieved after some time to hear the welcome accents of a Sergeant and Private of the Royal Scots Infantry, who said they had watched the encounter and that 'one of theirs' had also crashed.

"14 May, late evening. Cleaned up in a field dressing post — with flying boot cut off and leg bandaged. Small flesh wound on my arm and a cut on the chin. I was taken during the night to a railhead at Nivove.

"15 May, am. General anaesthetic was given to straighten my leg and put it in a splint. During the operation the glass roof of the station waiting-room being used as an emergency theatre was smashed during a bombing raid.

"16 May. Left Nivove on a hospital train and had frequent stops because of dive bombing.

"17 May, pm. I had arrived at Dieppe after nearly two days on the train, which covered less than 200 miles. After being taken from the train I was put in the Casino on the seafront which was being used as a military hospital. At the hospital I met Pilot Officer Trevor Jay, who had an arm wound; he was later to join 87 Squadron. There was a bombing raid on Dieppe that night and the Casino was damaged.

"18 May. My leg was placed in plaster. A mistake as the wound was still bleeding; and after a few days the wound began to stink.

"19 May. Evacuated from the wrecked Casino to a hospital 10 miles outside of Dieppe.

"21 May, am. Loaded onto an ambulance with three other stretcher cases plus two infantry officers with arm wounds (Sherwood Foresters and Black Watch) and then taken to Dieppe Harbour to be put on a hospital ship for home. Later that day Dieppe had taken several more bombing raids and the hospital ship was set on fire and two ambulances were destroyed. I was taken from the burning hospital ship to a railway station which had trains burning fiercely. The Black Watch officer drew his revolver and forced the reluctant French driver to take us to Rouen. The journey took five hours as the roads were crammed with civilian refugees. Frequent stops and starts which were painful as no medical orderly was in the ambulance. The two army chaps collected flower vases from a florist shop in Rouen for our relief! We had some difficulty getting petrol but eventually found a French fuel dump. No other ambulances were with us and we had no idea where to go. The French police suggested Evreux, 30 miles to the south of Rouen: this meant an overnight journey.

"22 May. We arrived at Evreux at dawn and could not find any British units, so we unloaded briefly from the ambulance and were cleaned up by some Nuns in a convent. They told us that there was a British hospital at Le Mans and that the roads were now clear of traffic. Thirty hours later we arrived at Le Mans and on the 26 May arrived at Southampton. On the 22 May, I had my leg amputated due to gangrene."

Whilst 'Dimmy' Joyce was making his way across France, the remainder of the squadron moved, on the 15th, to Lille-Marc, which immediately came under attack from 200 aircraft. No 87 Squadron were in no condition to mount any defence and stayed on the ground. On this day the Dutch capitulated and Paris was in a state of panic when news reached there, that Sedan had fallen. French Premier Reynaud telephoned Churchill to say "We are beaten; we have lost the battle!"

Flight Lieutenant Garry Nowell had a most eventful day on 16 May, as he has cause to remember.

"On 16 May, a squadron fresh from England with a full quota of aircraft arrived at the station and announced their intention of taking over the remainder of No 87 Squadron's aircraft. The CO of No 87 Squadron forcibly declined, but was unable to get the newly-arrived squadron leader to adopt his suggestion of handing over his aircraft to No 87 Squadron. After some discussion it was decided to put up a composite flight of six aircraft, including the three serviceable machines from No 87 Squadron. Dennis David and Flying Officer Saunders plus myself manned the three machines. Our first action was to attack aircraft raiding a nearby Belgian town. There was low cloud and Dennis David went below it and was fired on by anti-aircraft guns, he climbed through the clouds again and discovered that although his two colleagues were with him, the remaining aircraft from the new squadron had disappeared. We then saw nine enemy aircraft. David and myself attacked, David broke off the attack but I pressed on and shot down the left hand rear aircraft of the enemy formation. I was unable to see where Dennis David had gone, so I attacked on my own, using a variety of attacks against the eight remaining enemy aircraft. I dived through the formation, attacked from port side — head on and from the rear. I am hazy about how many aircraft were left after this exercise but I remember the uncanny silence which prevailed before I noticed that enemy flare had shot my propeller off. I immediately made a force landing in the nearest suitable field, narrowly missing a road crowded with civilian refugees. After landing the Hurricane safely, I tried setting the aircraft on fire by firing my revolver into the petrol tank, but nothing resulted. At this stage I saw approaching a stranger in a military uniform, also carrying a revolver. This proved to be a Belgian Lieutenant who spoke good English and took me to the small nearby village of Goefradinge. From there the obliging Belgian took me by car to the nearest railway station which was Louvain, bought a ticket to Brussels, I was shown the platform and then put on the train. The train started and travelled at walking pace for about three miles, then it was stopped by the Gendarme who, after consultation with the guard and looking along the train, ordered me to disembark. The Gendarme took charge, escorted me to the police station across the field and got a notebook out and started asking me questions, regarding where I'd been and where I was intent on going. I told him that I was from France and asked if I could ring the squadron for confirmation to be arranged with the Gendarme. While the Gendarme was conversing with someone over the telephone I noticed a convoy of army vehicles passing and quickly ran from the room and mounted one of the passing vehicles. After a hasty explanation to a British officer in charge of the convoy I was given transport to the headquarters of General Montgomery where, after another explanation to a staff officer, I was driven back to the squadron in a staff car. This took all night through roads packed with refugees and with all sorts of vehicles, motorised, horse drawn and even donkey drawn.

When I reported back to the squadron in the early morning I was greeted with great surprise as, when Dennis David had returned alone I had been reported missing. Later that day I wrote out my report on the previous day's combat and claimed one enemy aircraft destroyed and four probably destroyed, I found out later that the squadron records had credited me with five enemy aircraft destroyed. It was about this time that the war correspondents for the various daily papers seized on the fact that I had become the top scoring pilot and invented the name for me of "Two Plane" Nowell, because of the two incidents in which I had shot down two aircraft on one flight. RAF policy was not to publish the scores of individual pilots, but to claim all credits on behalf of the team comprising the squadron, but newspapers picked my title and alleged nick names and I was featured prominently in a number of dailies."

German troops entered Brussels on 17 May, and General Guderian was reprimanded by his superiors for his excessive speed and the extent of his advance. At this, Guderian resigned in protest, only to be 'persuaded' that evening to reverse his decision. Despite the action around Brussells this day, No 87 Squadron were not in action but acted as escort to several sorties of Blenheims to Couvain and Tournai.

The following day, the 18th, saw No 87 Squadron's Hurricanes in combat again as the Luftwaffe continued to support the ground forces which took Antwerp and reached Cambrai. The day's action began for the squadron when Johnny Cock, on patrol with two others over the Coutral-Tournai sector, shot down one of 80 Ju 87s. Johnny Cock's victim fell into a wood and burst into flames. Later, four of the squadron's Hurricanes made an attack of a single Henschel Hs 126 observation aircraft which was spotted flying at 3,000 feet over Valenciennes. The four Hurricanes dived onto the slow flying machine and all overshot their target as its pilot pulled up steeply into a stall. Using the low speed handling qualities of his machine to advantage, the German pilot out manoeuvred his attackers until Flying Officer Ward first silenced the rear gunner and then sent the Henschel down in flames. Ward noted, ''The Luftwaffe crew of this Henschel put up a first class show.'' The day ended with another loss to the squadron when Pilot Officer G. C. Saunders was shot down and killed over Lille.

That evening, the continuous sound of exploding bombs, anti-aircraft fire and air raid sirens made sleep almost impossible but, at dawn on the 19th, all the Hurricanes were ordered off.

Flying Officer Ward was one of the pilots. 'We all took off in a panic climb from Lille aerodrome. AA guns directed us to enemy aircraft, about nine Me 109s, and a free for all developed. I was in a steep right hand turn when I saw an Me 109 attacking a Hurricane about 4,000 feet below. I dived and attacked the enemy aircraft who broke away and carried out evasive tactics, his coolant tank began to pour out smoke. I broke off the engagement as I mistook a Hurricane coming up behind me as an Me 109. Two Hurricanes continued to fire at the same aircraft. I followed with a final

burst and when I last saw the 109 it was at ground level flying at about 140 mph over the lines.'' Flying Officer 'Dicky' Glyde reported attacking an Me 109, south of Lille, but run out of ammunition before inflicting any great damage, he also reported that he had seen Pilot Officer Dunn shot down in flames. 'Widge' Gleed took off shortly after with two other Hurricane pilots in pursuit of five Me 109s which had just brought down two Lysanders. After a long chase, Gleed succeeded in firing all his ammunition into one Me 109 which was last seen at ground level and pouring smoke.

Just before noon, a convoy of lorries arrived at Lille bringing supplies, but one was missing, the lorry carrying rations had been struck by a bomb during the night and destroyed. 'Widge' Gleed and 'Roddy' Rayner then took off in pursuit of an He 111 near Orchies. After making simultaneous stern and quarter attacks, one crew man baled out and the Heinkel dived into the ground and exploded. Half an hour later, at 12.30 hours, Gleed led 12 other Hurricanes in an attack on 20 enemy aircraft which had been identified as Dornier Do 215s. Although it is believed that several of the enemy were brought down, no record has survived of this combat. Similarly, there are no details of the afternoon's engagement between a force of over 20 Hurricanes and a similar number of Dorniers, although both sides suffered casualties.

Six replacement Hurricanes were sent from Amiens ready for operations on 20 May. Some of the pilots had come straight form Flight Training Schools and some had never flown Hurricanes before. In the confusion of the moment, neither pilot's names nor aircraft serial numbers were recorded. Only two of the new pilots, Flying Officer Ward and Pilot Officer Comeley survived to tell their story, the fate of the others is not known.

On an early patrol over Douai, at 05.00 hours, Pilot Officer Comeley brought down a Ju 88 and later in the day brought down another over Roubaix. As patrols and interceptions continued, the squadron moved bases back to

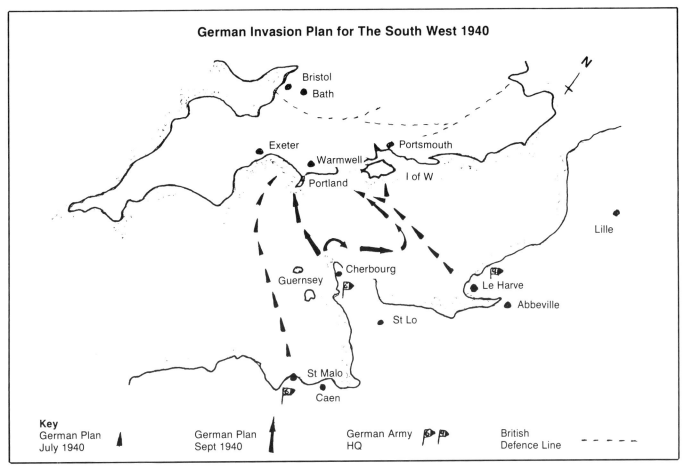

German Invasion Plan for The South West 1940

Key
German Plan July 1940
German Plan Sept 1940
German Army HQ
British Defence Line

Merville, from where 'Widge' Gleed and Pilot Officer Ken Tait took off to intercept more Ju 88s over Douai. After a long chase the two pilots managed to bring one bomber down in flames at 07.00 hours. At 10.00 hours, white shell bursts from anti aircraft guns were seen close to the airfield and bombs fell close by. Several of the squadron's pilots scrambled in pursuit and one of the bombers was claimed as destroyed. In the afternoon, the retreating troops which had been seen passing Lille came streaming past Merville. A young French officer told that Arras had fallen and the Germans were advancing to the coast. A captain, in charge of a battery of 75 mm guns, related the tale that General Gamelin had been executed by the Paris Mob and that the Germans were in Abbeville. Gamelin had not been executed, but dismissed and replaced by General Weygand as Allied Commander-in-Chief. Apart from this, the captain was right. The Germans had advanced 386 km in 11 days — it was unbelievable!

On the afternoon of 20 May, orders came to strafe troops on the Arras-Cambrai road. No sooner had the squadron sighted a convoy than they were 'bounced' by Me 109s. 'Widge' Gleed sought the safely of cloud and got on the tail of an Me 109 which he shot down east of Cambrai, before hedge hopping back to Merville. The situation was clearly critical and it was plain that the squadron must escape to England if they were to avoid being over-run by the German advance. Accordingly, orders were issued for all flyable machines to leave immediately for England and again Flying Officer Ward flew one of the Hurricanes.

"After being evacuated from Lille to Merville on Sunday evening, owing to the advance of the enemy, I landed at Merville at 16.00 hours on Monday, 20 May. I was ordered to fly an unserviceable Hurricane home to Debden. This machine had no gunsight and all the instruments, except the compass, oil temp. and pressure guages were U/S. The engine was badly over-heating and the oil temperature at minus one boost was 98°C. Seven guns were loaded but there was no incendiary or tracer to help with my aim.

I intended to land at Abbeville to collect some kit which I had left there on the way out. On approaching Abbeville I saw that the town was in flames and three Dornier 215s were dive-bombing the town. I climbed and attacked one of the three enemy aircraft and got in three bursts at 300 yards, without a gunsight, pointing my machine in the general direction of the aircraft. The Dornier dived into cloud, I followed and gave the enemy some more bursts in the cloud. I came out of cloud, circled for 10 minutes and saw another Do 215 between clouds and attacked again. My engine began to over-heat badly and 109s attacked me from behind. I dived into cloud and eventually landed at Abbeville.

I found that the Hurricane had a punctuare in the starboard tank and the petrol was spraying out. The aerodrome was being evacuated and the U/S machines were being burned, chiefly Lysanders. The aerodrome crews were about to evacuate and they wished to burn my Hurricane rather than take the risk of starting it again owing to the petrol spraying out of the starboard tank. I struck a bayonet several times

Flying Officer Derek Ward with his aircraft at Exeter in July, 1940. Note the extra large roundel caused by adding a yellow outer to the existing A type roundel as originally carried. Name 'Kia Ora' is painted below cockpit and a gyro gunsight is fitted.

into the starboard tank to empty it and managed to persuade two airmen to fill my port tank. I had to leave without the starboard tank being repaired and with only 50 rounds in each of the seven guns. I took off from Abbeville and two miles east of the aerodrome I encountered six Do 17s and six Me 109s. I attacked the leader of the 109s, which were coming head-on towards me, and I gave the leader a burst. He swerved left and I dived past him towards the ground. Fortunately the 109 continued on, escorting the bombers, and did not give chase. I flew my Hurricane over the Channel and landed at North Weald, England."

The ground crews were left at Merville and waited anxiously for the transport aircraft to ferry them out. Eventually, two DC-2 airliners from the Dutch KLM airline, still in civil markings, landed. Within 15 minutes all were on their way, leaving behind all their kit and equipment on the now deserted airfield.

In 11 days the squadron had lost six pilots and 11 machines. This does not take into account the ferry pilots and other unknown men who were killed whilst flying Hurricanes marked with the No 87 Squadron code letters 'LK'.

No 87 Squadron pilots killed in the Battle of France:

Flying Officer Campbell	Shot down over Brussels
Pilot Officer Mackworth	Shot down over Brussels
Pilot Officer Edwards	Shot down over Brussels
Pilot Officer Saunders	Shot down over Lille
Pilot Officer Eryse	Shot down over Le Chateau
Pilot Officer Orgood	Shot down over Marstricht

On the following day, in a speech to the Senate, Premier Reynaud said:

"France cannot die! . . . . If I were told tomorrow that only a miracle could save France, I should reply, 'I believe in miracles because I believe in France!'"

'Dinky' Howell retired from the RAF in 1947, after 14 years in the service, to join the Atomic Energy Research Establishment at Winfrith, Dorset, where he took up the post of Senior Experimental Officer. He retired in 1981, and began to compile his autobiography. Some of his memoirs feature within these pages but regretably, just weeks after dictating his accounts of the Battle of France to his sons, he passed away.

'Roddy' Rayner, whose full name was Roderick Malachi Seaburne Rayner, had joined the RAF before the outbreak of war and flew all his fighter operations with No 87 Squadron. Later in 1941, he was awarded the DFC but made no further fighter claims. He died in 1982.

Dennis David, became a flight commander of No 213 Squadron,

in October 1940, and moved on to No 152 Squadron before being posted to the Middle East in 1943. Here he commanded No 89 Squadron and was promoted to Group Captain, remaining in Ceylon and Burma to the war's end as Senior Air Staff Officer of No 224 Group. From 1945 to his retirement in 1967, he held many challenging and demanding posts such as the Honorary Aide to Viscount Trenchard from 1955 to the death of the 'Father of the RAF' in 1956. His next assignment was as His Majesty's Air Attaché in Budapest. During the Hungarian uprising, he was responsible for assisting over 400 people to escape the Hungarian and Russian Secret Police. He was later knighted by the Grand Duke of Hapsburg, the exiled hereditary Royal Ruler of Hungary. Today, Dennis lives with his wife, Margaret, in London and spends much of his time travelling the world and lecturing on the RAF.

'A' Flight commander Gleed in good old 'A', photographed by 'Watty' Watson while en route to Portland in August 1940 at the height of the Battle of Britain. LK-A was aircraft P2798, and Gleed had Figaro the cat painted below the cockpit on the starboard side.

3. Britain on her own

As the personnel of No 87 Squadron gathered at Debden and later Church Fenton, the final collapse of mainland Europe took place. The people of Britain and the members of the No 87 Squadron prepared to face the onslaught of Germany's military might which, as yet, no army had been able to resist for long.

Whilst the British people, perhaps stirred by the speeches of Churchill, began to equip themselves with whatever weapons were at hand, the RAF began to replace some of the 931 aircraft which had been lost in France. Of this total, 453 were fighters, the majority of these Hurricanes, leaving Britain deficient of front line fighters. The tattered remains of the British Army which had been evacuated from Dunkirk and the Local Defence Volunteers could, no doubt, have put up a spirited defence of the country had an invasion force crossed the Channel. But, without air superiority there could be no invasion; if the RAF could control the airspace over the British coast then there could be no invasion. The tools by which this could be achieved were fighters and these were in short supply. During June and July, a total of 591 Hurricanes and 265 Spitfires were built, supplementing the survivors of France and Dunkirk.

With a numerical disadvantage in men and machines, their efficient use was of the upmost importance. Radio Direction Finding, later called Radar, provided the 'eyes' at long range enabling fighters to be positioned with reasonably accuracy to meet an incoming force. Over land, the Royal Observer Corps provided more accurate information on the position and height of both enemy and RAF forces. Information from all sources was gathered at control centres and from there fighters were controlled. No 87 Squadron came under the control of 10 Group, which was responsible for an area from Land's End to Southampton and across to the Welsh Borders.

Brought up to operational strength again by the addition of new pilots and machines, the squadron moved to Exeter with 14 Hurricanes on 4 June 1940. During the re-equipping no sorties were made but, on 6 July, Pilot Officer Dunn, survivor of the Battle of France, was killed in a flying accident at Yeadon. When the squadron arrived at Exeter, they had been beaten to the best accommodation by the men

of No 213 Squadron, who had moved in two weeks before them. The officers of the squadron were billeted at the Rougemont Hotel in Exeter and the men at Farrington House, not far from the airfield. The ground crews, as usual, got the worst of the accommodation.

Only five days passed before the squadron found itself in action. On 9 July, Sergeant Cowley had an inconclusive engagement with an He 111 from which sections of engine cowling were seen to fall before it was lost in cloud 10 miles south of Portland.

On 11 July, No 87 Squadron had its first opportunity to engage a large enemy formation over Britain. About 18 Ju

Servicing LK-G at Exeter in July, 1940, showing the panel over the machine gun muzzles removed. Notice exhaust staining and worn paintwork. Also visible is the bead sight on the cowling top.

87s from III/StG 2 were approaching Portland, with an escort of forty Me 110s from III/ZG76. As the formation approached, RDF at Ventnor on the Isle of Wight alerted 11 Group which sent No 601 Squadron. From 10 Group, came three Hurricanes on No 87 Squadron, the pilots found themselves in a position to attack 12 of the Me 110s as Squadron Leader 'Johnny' Dewar reported.

"Leading flight of three Hurricanes at 5,000 feet west of Weymouth, sighted nine enemy aircraft approaching Portland from south at 15,000 feet approx. Commenced to climb going south to get in between enemy aircraft and sun. Saw nine more enemy aircraft and one group of about 12 Me 110s as we were going up. Got level and up-sun of enemy at about 12,000 feet. As we approached, some aircraft dived on shipping which were in Portland Harbour. Enemy did not appear to be aware of our presence. Saw two other Hurricanes attacking and swung into Me 110s which seemed to be trying to form a circle. Saw a Hurricane diving and turning slowly with Me 110 on his tail; put first burst into Me 110. On last burst port engine appeared to blow up. Aircraft flicked on to its back and dived almost vertically. Owing to presence of numerous enemy aircraft I did not watch aircraft crash.

"Having disposed of one Me 110, I went into full turn to review progress of battle and to remove two other enemy aircraft trying to get on my tail. Saw a bomb exploding by shipping in the harbour and two enemy aircraft diving for ground. One Me 110 still pursuing me. The Hurricane turned easily on to his tail, he was vertically banked. He then dived for ground going east − I followed but withheld fire as I was getting short of rounds. Me 110 pulled out about 1,000 feet and continued in 'S' turns. I gave him a burst from about 100 yards and vapour came out of both engines. I had to slam throttle back to avoid over-shooting, vapour then ceased to come from engines and he gathered away again. I was very close and saw no rear gun fire, so held my position and took careful non-deflective shot using all my ammunition. Me 110 at once turned inland going very slowly. Seeing me draw away he turned seaward again. I went to head him off and he, apparently thinking I had more rounds, turned for land again sinking slowly. At about 200 feet another Hurricane came up and fired a short burst at him. He immediately turned and landed on Grange Heath near Wareham, Dorset. Both crew got out wearing yellow jackets. Army were close by, number of other Hurricane was UW-F (I think)."

Flying Officer 'Dicky' Glyde brought down another Me 110 which landed on the sea, east of Portland Bill and had a lucky escape when a bullet pierced the central panel of his hood and struck the armour plate at the back of his head. Pilot Officer Jay also shot down an Me 110, which he saw dive into the sea at a speed of over 300 mph.

Oberleutnant Gerhard Kadow, Staffelkapitän of 9/ZG76, was the pilot of one of the Me 110s.

"As I approached the English Coast, I was confronted with the enemy. I counted about 20 dark dots in the distance, somewhat higher than myself. As they came nearer, I was certain they were British fighters, though I could not see if they were Spitfires or Hurricanes.

"I knew that the twin engined Me 110 was not as manoeuvrable as these fighters and that there was little chance of winning a battle with them, especially as there were only seven Me 110s in my staffel and we were out numbered three to one. Our orders, however, were to defend the Stukas and so we must engage the enemy.

"Our offensive armament consisted of two 20 mm cannon and 7.92 mm machine guns in the nose, so I made a head-on attack. I pressed the gun buttons and a stream of bullets flew out like water from a hose pipe. Our closing speed very high and we both broke away to avoid collision.

"In the next moment, two fighters were behind me and firing. My engines stopped and I knew that returning to France was impossible. The fighters followed me down and stopped firing, they could see what trouble I was in. I jettisoned my cockpit hood in the hope that it might hit one of the fighters but rather obviously this failed! I ordered Helmut Scholz to do the same but he reported that his hood was damaged and jammed, now we could not bale out and ditching in the sea was not advisable as Helmut might not be able to get out before the machine sank.

"I decided that I must make a forced landing, which I did rather well on Povington Heath, near Wareham at about 12.45 hours. I then discovered that I could not leave the aircraft immediately because a bullet had blown a hole in my seat and the sharp edges had been forced into my parachute pack. I pulled forward and got out to help Helmut, who had been injured by splinters.

"Now I must destroy my aircraft. At this time we had no demolition device fitted, so I tried to set light to the fuel tanks by firing my pistol into them. I used all eight rounds but failed, perhaps just as well as I think it would have exploded and killed us both!

"As I was trying to destroy the aircraft I could hear gun fire and bullets hitting it. I went round the aircraft to see where the bullets were coming from and was hit in the heel of my boot, the bullet bounced off the rubber and left me with only a flesh wound. Both of us left the aircraft well alone and looked around to see about 20 soldiers getting up, an officer ordered 'hands up' and took us prisoner. I later told him that it was unfair to shoot aircrew who had been shot down, but he said that he was trying to prevent us destroying our aircraft and I should be glad that I hadn't been shot dead."

This was certainly the Me 110 that 'Johnny' Dewar had

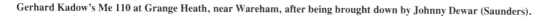

Gerhard Kadow's Me 110 at Grange Heath, near Wareham, after being brought down by Johnny Dewar (Saunders).

51270 Leutnant SCHRÖDER Joachim.

Above: Leutnant Schröder is picked up from the sea off Portland (top left) and taken by Navy launch (top right) into seven years of captivity (left). The gunner of Schröder's Me 110, Gefreiter Sorokoput (above) was not as lucky as his pilot and lost his life (Saunders).

Gerhard Kadow (centre) photographed in a Canadian POW camp in 1941 (Saunders).

had a hand in bringing down. Other Me 110s that were brought down were that of Oberleutnant Göring, whose machine dived vertically into The Verne, near Portland Harbour and that of Leutnant Schröder, which landed on the sea off Ney Breakwater. A fourth machine, flown by Leutnant Graf zu Castell, is believed to have dived into the sea somewhere off Portland.

Naturally enough, the three pilots returned, jubilant, to Exeter after the squadron's first large scale combat over Britain. Later this day, Squadron Leader 'Johnny' Dewar was posted to the position of Officer Commanding RAF Exeter, his place in No 87 Squadron was taken by Squadron Leader Lovell-Gregg. A period of inactivity followed, during which 'A' Flight made some night patrols from Hullavington. On 19 July, Sergeant Thorogood lost the other aircraft in his section and found himself behind eight Ju 87s flying just west of Portland. 'Rubber' Thorogood made a rear attack and silenced one of the rear gunners before return fire from the remaining Stukas forced him to break off his lone attack.

Pilot Officer 'Bea' Beamont was at readiness at Exeter on the morning of 24 July when, as he recalls, the order came to scramble.

"I was scrambled on interception patrol from Exeter on a glorious summer morning. Climbing our Hurricanes initially towards the North Devon Coast through scattered cumulus clouds tinged orange at the tops by the sunrise, it was to a 19 year old, wonderful to be alive and difficult to contemplate the sombre reason for being there. Stable anti-cyclonic conditions with good visibility below cloud and unlimited above presented no weather difficulties for this patrol. My Hurricane LK-L, was familiar and comforting in it's steady instrument readings and engine note. As we levelled at 10,000 feet above Barnstable the orange-gold of the eastern skyline merged into deep purple above, fading into the delicate pale hues of the far distant horizon. Below, the land and sea of the Severn estuary lay indistinct in misty mauve shadow between the golden clouds. But we were on

serious business and the controller, for once intelligible in our TR9 headsets, in pressing tones instructed that we should turn onto 260° and 'Buster' (the code for increase speed) after a positively identified 'Bandit'.

"Thirty seconds later he gave warning of other fighters intercepting and then said, 'Bandit dead ahead of you at two miles, probably below you.' We were turning slightly to the left over Lundy Isle when I saw a dark speck against the haze between two brilliant orange patches of cumulus and calling, 'Aircraft 10 o'clock low' I rolled in towards it at full throttle and fine pitch. The aircraft was tracking across from right to left and I had an impression of the high square tail of a Ju 87; but it had no spatted undercarriage and I could see twin engines — a Ju 88. With twin streams of thin smoke it was going fast in a shallow dive southwards towards Devon and then from the right a Spitfire appeared firing at quite long range before pulling away and up to starboard.

I assumed that he had finished his ammunition and so continued at full bore until after what seemed a long interval to close the gap, I was in firing position at about 300 yards dead astern and in the turbulence of the enemy's wake. We

Schröder's Me 110 pictured in June, 1940 (Saunders).

Below: Oberleutnant Göring, nephew of the Luftwaffe chief Herman Göring, and Oberleutnant Zimmerman were aboard an Me 110 which fell vertically from the sky at great speed to bury itself in the ground near the naval base. Little more than a smoking hole marks their passing and no traces of their bodies were recovered. Above: The exact spot as it is today.

Lynton, a young lad of only 10 was working on his father's farm when the Ju 88 came sailing overhead. Smoke was pouring from the aircraft and RAF fighters were still chasing it, the aircraft at once started to land only 800 yards from the farm, it bounced a few times before ploughing through a hedgerow.

Later that day three pilots turned up at the crash site to inspect their kill and to remove the swastika from the tail section which did not burn out with the rest of the aircraft. The tail section had to be turned upside down to allow the pilots to cut out the panel. They later drove through Martinhoe in an open top car with this panel held high over their heads, to the delight of the locals.

The following day, 25 July, 'Roddy' Rayner made an

were both doing about 320 mph in a steepening dive and I fired a long burst from my Hurricane's eight 303 machine guns and saw some return fire. The 88 lurched, streamed more smoke and the starboard propeller slowed down. Now, down below 1,000 feet, we crossed the coast north of Barnstable and as the German slowed I held fire because he seemed to be going for a forced landing. Suddenly an object separated from his fuselage and the rear gunner fell past with a glimpse of white his parachute streamed at a very low height. Then, as I was struggling to stay behind him, the 88 slowed right down and slithered across a field and up a heather slope into a hedge in a cloud of dust.

''Breaking sharply round to port through a patch of low early morning mist, I turned back over the field to see a puff of oily black smoke and orange flames as the wreck ignited. There was no sign of life and I had momentary fear that the rest of the crew were trapped in the flames, but the second time round and at a very low level I could see one man pulling another away from the cockpit and they were soon lying on the ground some distance from the burning wreck.

''To complete the scene a battered Morris truck coming down the nearest lane proved to be the local Home Guard unit arriving to do their duty. I waved to them and then set course for Exeter where I landed to find that I had seen the 88 much earlier than the other two members of the section who had been unable to catch up after not following me initially. In accord with practice of the time I reported the engagement to the station intelligence section but did not claim a victory as it was assumed that the first attacker, the Spitfire, should have the credit. With the pressure of events that summer and subsequently, more than a decade was to pass before I learnt that the Spitfire had been flown by Bob Stanford-Tuck, one of the top scoring pilots of the period, operating from Pembrey.''

On this day Master Dalyn of Killmington Farm, near

Above: Although shot down by Beamont, three pilots from 92 Squadron, P/Os Bryson, Paterson and Kingcombe, remove the Swastika with the aid of tin snips. Mr.Dalyn's father is climbing over the gate, extreme left (Saunders).

Below: The same site, 48 years on, with the gap in the hedge caused by the crashing aircraft still remaining.

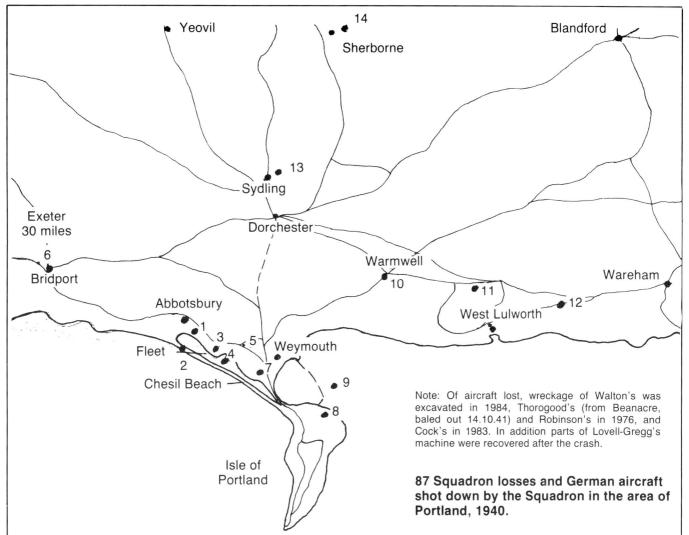

Note: Of aircraft lost, wreckage of Walton's was excavated in 1984, Thorogood's (from Beanacre, baled out 14.10.41) and Robinson's in 1976, and Cock's in 1983. In addition parts of Lovell-Gregg's machine were recovered after the crash.

87 Squadron losses and German aircraft shot down by the Squadron in the area of Portland, 1940.

Key: 1. S/Ldr Lovell-Gregg 15.8.40. Killed in action; 2. Me 109 shot down by Tait 25.8.40. Pilot Hptmn Maculan killed; 3. Sgt Wakeling 25.8.40. Killed in action; 4. P/O Cock 11.8.40. Wounded, baled out; 5. Me 109 shot down by Beamont 25.8.40. Pilot Gefr Broeker safe; 6. Sgt Cowley force landed after combat 15.8.40. Pilot wounded; 7. P/O Jay force landed after combat 13.8.40. Pilot safe; 8. Me 110 shot down by Dewar 11.7.40. Crew Oblt Goering and Oblt Zimmerman both killed in action; 9. Me 110 shot down by Glyde 11.7.40. Crew L/T Schroder rescued from sea, Gefr Sorokoput killed; 10. P/O Mclure force landed after combat 11.8.40. Pilot safe; 11. Messerschmitt 110 shot down by Dewar 25.8.40. Crew Lt Westphal and Obergefr Brief both killed; 12. Me 110 shot down by Dewar 11.7.40. Crew Oblt Kadow and Gefr Scholz safe; 13. Me 109 shot down by Cock 30.9.40. Pilot Uffz Gollinger killed; 14. Sgt Walton 30.9.40. Baled out wounded. F/O Glyde killed in action 13.8.40. Lost at sea off Portland. Sgt Comeley killed in action 15.8.40. Lost at sea off Portland. P/O Vose-Jeff killed in action 11.8.40. Lost at sea off Portland.

attack on an Me 110 which he last saw diving away with its starboard engine on fire. As it was not seen to crash, Rayner could only claim it as a 'probable' but as the combat was some 20 miles south-west of Portland it was considered unlikely that a safe return could have been made.

'B' Flight moved to Hullavington, situated to the north of Bath, on 26 July to carry out night patrols. Fitter, Reg Guppy, went with them.

"I recall a little ditty of the war years which went something like, 'The little dicky birds they fly by day and go to roost at night, but the Hurrybirds they fly by day and all the bloody night.'

"We were told that 'B' Flight would leave Exeter and proceed to Hullavington. This was to be another of our oh so regular jaunts. We arrived to find ourselves at a flying school and part of RAF Flying Training Command.

There was something about flying training schools and fighter squadrons that did not see eye-to-eye.

"We were billeted in old married quarters as far from the camp as possible, but as this accommodation made a welcome change to the tents which we occupied, we were not going to complain, even if it was decidedly cramped. We had the feeling that the training bods did not want us to comtaminate their pupils, or maybe it was the thought that we might not have changed our socks?.

"It was now the vogue for all fighter types to keep the top button of their jackets undone and by their standards we were a bit scruffy, but since we lived for the most part like gypies perhaps it's not surprising.

"Our kites were dispersed a fair distance from the training mob so there was no real conflict. The kites that were being used for training were old two seater biplane Hawker Harts. These were only used in the daytime. They also had Oxford twin-engined trainers that were used for night flying.

"We were soon to find out what we were there for. We were to start night flying 'tomorrow' — just like that. I don't recall any dummy run, special instructions or night flying equipment. There may have been the odd torch produced for the occasion but that was about all. Only a few had been on night flying exercises before but that was far different in peace time, when the whole place was lit up like Blackpool, all this was to be carried out in the pitch dark.

"For anyone who has not experienced leading an aircraft in at night, in the pitch dark with only a torch for the pilot to see where to go and you running like hell with a bloody great kite taxiing twice as fast as you can run, it is not an experience I would recommend to the faint-hearted.

"I don't recall being issued with cat's eyes either. The thought of being hit by a revolving prop. didn't bear thinking about.

"On the appointed day we reversed the procedure and in-

A WAAF driver helps the war economy by liberating some fuel from Georg Strickstrock's Heinkel 111 which crashed at Honiton (Foote).

stead of having the kite ready for dawn we got them ready for dusk. I do not recall just how many kites were detailed for the first night's operation, but the first away was an NCO pilot, Sgt Culverwell.

"As this was a new experience, we were all pretty much on our toes and as the kites taxied out to take off one at a time, we all stood around the dispersal to watch. The first kite took off OK along the runway and we watched him climb away as his rear light located on the rudder could clearly be seen, but what seemed strange was his very steep rate of climb, far steeper than a normal take off. After a while we were to see the lights of his kite, both navigation lights heading for the deck, this was followed by an explosion and fire. We were dumbfounded at this sight, we were all shook rigid. However, by now other kites were getting airborne in a more normal manner.

"The Form 700 was immediately impounded, as was the custom on the occasion of a lost kite, but night flying was to continue.

"We continued the programme of night flying without further incident except that 'chiefy' had to attend a board of enquiry, and we had to give our account of what happened. As we all saw exactly the same from the ground, it was generally felt by us non-pilots that he took off and climbed too steeply and stalled into the ground , but as we did not hear the findings of the enquiry this can only be conjecture."

Later on the same night, Johnny Cock sighted an He 111 over Portishead, near Bristol at 23.30 hours. The bomber was held in the cone of Bristol's searchlights and Cock wasted no time in attacking from below. The starboard engine stopped and the aircraft started to loose height in a south westerly direction before Cock lost sight of the Heinkel which crashed some five minutes later at Smeathorpe near Honiton. Pilot of the 1/KG4 Heinkel, was Georg Strickstrock who was the only man aboard to bale out successfully.

"We were flying high, having dropped two magnetic mines near Barry Docks and were on our way home. I can remember a sudden thud and I lost power completely, the 'plane went out of control within a very short while. The only other thing I could remember was parachuting to earth."

The final incident of July, which the squadron thought of note, occured on the 28th, when Pilot Officer Darwin collided with another Hurricane at Exeter and was taken to Exeter Hospital suffering head injuries.

In 1981 Georg Strickstrock and his wife visited the site and stand at exactly the spot (upper picture) where his Heinkel crashed. The lady in the centre is Mrs Bull, who was one of the first to reach the crashed plane back in 1940 (Hood).

Flying Officer R. F. Watson of 87 Squadron beside his Hurricane 1 in August, 1940. In this very typical Battle of Britain scene. 'Watty' Watson is wearing his Mae West lifejacket over his uniform, the starter trolley is plugged into the aircraft and fabric patchs cover the gun ports (Watson).

'Watty' Watson died in 1986, he was one of the first members of the squadron that the author had the honour to meet. His life-long hobby was photography and it is by no accident that many of the photographs in this book were taken by him. His other hobby was making model aircraft, he had done it throughout the Battle of Britain and carried on to pass his interests on to son and grandson who continue the tradition.

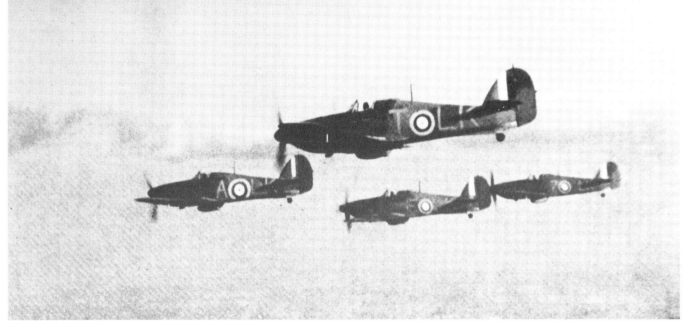

The Hurricanes of 'Widge' Gleed, Ken Tait, Dinky Howell and Roger Malengreau, on patrol in August, 1940 and caught in formation by 'Watty' Watson who photographed them from his own Hurricane (Watson).

4. High Activity

Four of No 87 Squadron's pilots made the journey from Exeter to Buckingham Palace on 5 August, the reason being the investiture of their decorations by the King. Squadron Leader 'Johnny' Dewar, Flying Officer 'Dicky' Glyde, Flight Lieutenant Vose-Jeff and Pilot Officer Dennis David all received Distinguished Flying Crosses.

Pilot Officer Comeley made a claim for an He 111 destroyed on the night of 8 August, he reported that the bomber crashed into the sea.

As the Luftwaffe began to increase the tempo of their raids over Britain, No 87 Squadron was on the verge of a period of activity as fierce as those of the Battle of France, three months before. The Radio Direction Finding stations along the south coast began to detect the approach of a large formation of 'Bandits'. At 10.05 hours on 11 August, the plotting tables of Fighter Command began once more to record the enemy's movements over the Channel. After initial engagements off Dover early in the day a significant number of aircraft began to appear form the Baie de la Seine area, between Cherbourg and Le Havre. At 10.05 hours the following forces had been identified:

30 + enemy aircraft thirty miles south of St. Catherine's point.
50 + enemy aircraft fifteen miles north of Cherbourg
9 + enemy aircraft twenty six miles north-west of Cherbourg

During the previous weeks the main targets to receive the still jubilant Luftwaffe's attentions were the many small convoys plying the Channel. On this day, however, there were no convoys to attract a force of such magnitude. Only the prominent naval base of Portland lay in the path of the advancing aircraft. Almost immediately the controllers of 10 and 11 Groups began to dispatch their forces to patrol the Portland area. Nos 1, 145 and 609 took off first, followed by 601, 152, 213, 238 and lastly 87 Squadron at 10.10 hours — a total of about 70 aircraft.

609 Squadron's twelve Spitfires were the first to encounter the enemy, a large number of Bf 110s of ZG2 and Bf 109s from JG2 south of Swanage. 609 Squadron made a diving attack out of the sun at the circling Bf 110s, five being

claimed as destroyed, 601 and 145 Squadrons then joined the combat but were to lose six aircraft and their pilots in an engagement with what appears to have been a decoy fighter force. The main bomber formation was by now approaching Portland Bill unmolested. Only the eight Hurricanes of 213 Squadron were able to engage the Ju 88s of KG 54 before their bombs began to fall.

On the ground the various gun batteries under command of the 5th Anti-Aircraft Division looked on as two formations approached Portland from the east and west. The Ju 88s dived down from 15,000 feet to between 100 and 500 feet approaching in a series of waves, bombing and machine gunning as they went.

The Verne Citadel and oil tanks of the naval base appeared to be the main targets. Two of the tanks caught fire, the resulting pall of smoke hampering the anti-aircraft gunners as further aircraft approached. Around the naval base itself a road leading to the Citadel was cratered and four small huts destroyed. A fire was started in the naval hospital but soon brought under control. Three hundred yards of railway track near HMS *Osprey* were demolished while further along the line the signal box at the entrance of Portland Station received a direct hit, the signalman being killed. In the harbour two small destroyers were hit, while damage was caused to the submarine school. Further afield 20 houses and a brewery were either demolished or nearly so while another 100 houses received damage of a minor nature from splinters and shrapnel.

Following the bombing, Nos 1 and 152 Squadrons engaged the fighter escort whilst 238 Squadron went for the Ju 88s, followed a few minutes later by the six Hurricanes of 87 Squadron's 'B' Flight: Pilot Officer Mclure, Pilot Officer Cock, Flight Sergeant Badger, Flying Officer Glyde, Flight Lieutenant Jeff and Pilot Officer David.

Dennis David still recalls vividly the awesome sight of this phalanx of planes, the largest formation yet seen over Britain: "There didn't seem much that we could do against this force, but we made to attack the Ju 88s as they turned away from Portland."

Before any of the pilots could make their attack, a group

'Widge's' good old 'A' with its ground crew. Note absence of serial (which was P2978), red of fin flash extended to leading edge of fin, the 'oversize' fuselage roundel and Figaro the cat painted below the cockpit canopy.

Below: 'A' Flight ground crews at Bibury in the summer of 1940, including Moore, Gotts, Manning, May, Worthington, Gregory, Hanny, Matthews, Everit, Henderson, Banham, Banks, Ashworth, Ward, Skeggs and Wynn.

of Bf 109s dived through the Hurricanes, breaking their line astern formation. Flight Sergeant Badger, flying as Blue Three, dived away after a 109 and was able to damage it with two short bursts of fire before another 109 attacked his own aircraft. During the brief dog fight which followed two bursts hit the 109, its engine stopped and petrol poured out. The aircraft spiralled down and was seen to crash into the sea.

Pilot Officer McLure, Green Two, went into a series of steep right hand turns and found himself out-turning one of the 109s. The Hurricane's fire hit the fighter and McLure watched it spinning into the sea. A number of the accompanying 109s then attacked McLure's aircraft. Their bullets struck home wounding McLure in the leg. The instruments were shot away and oil sprayed into the cockpit, covering its interior and the canopy.

McLure's combat report recalls what happened: ''I dived away steeply doing right hand aileron turns down to about 5,000 feet. The 109s did not follow me down. I headed for shore and was attacked by, I believe, He 112s. I again turned steeply to the right and got my sights on the rear enemy aircraft. I foliowed him down to thirty feet off the water and gave a burst of about two seconds. He seemed to lose control but oil covered my windshield and I was unable to see what happened.''

The other six aircraft continued to attack McLure's machine until he reached the coast where a wheels up forced landing was made near Warmwell.

John Cock's day had started well. A fellow pilot had repaid a long standing debt of £5, ''a considerable amount in

those days'' John recalls. ''With the fiver firmly in my trouser pocket I left Exeter and had little trouble in spotting the bombers. By then there were a total of about 200 of them spread out all over Portland. The first aircraft I shot at was a 109. I gave him several bursts and saw bits come flying off. He was obviously damaged and I doubt that he got very much further.

''I found the Ju 88 next and managed to get in behind him. One of my guns had already jammed but I carried on and fired off the rest of my ammunition. One of the wings was

Pilot Officer Mclure at the time of the action described here (Watson).

Five pilots at Exeter. Left to Right: 'Watty' Watson, Ken Tait, 'Widge' Gleed, Roddy Rayner and Peter Comeley, who was killed on August 15, 1940.

The Tiger Moth 'hack' used for communication flights, liaison and visits to girl friends! Ken Tait and 'Widge' stand by as Peter Comeley swings the prop, on a warm evening in July, 1940.

well alight but I didn't see the 88 crash as a line of bullets hit the left hand side of my cockpit. There was a dreadful din. The dash panel disintegrated and the engine began to run a bit rough. A bullet had nicked my left arm and other bits of shrapnel embedded themselves in it.

"The 109 that had hit me dived away and I saw two white bars on it. Later the Squadron Intelligence Officer told me that this was probably Helmut Wick. With my plane fairly badly hit I decided that this was no place to be, so I pulled back the hood and rolled the plane over. I tried to get out, but got stuck on something, so I kicked the stick forward and shot out into space. I grabbed the rip cord and pulled it. When the 'chute opened I was still hanging on to the handle for all I was worth. I put it in my jacket pocket and still keep it as a souvenir!

"Floating down I could see and hear the other aircraft whirling around. I felt a bit vulnerable, especially when my parachute cords fell around me. Another Me 109 was shooting at me! Dennis David got onto the 109 and I watched him shoot the aircraft down. The pilot didn't get out of that one.

"When I hit the water my 'chute began to drag me towards Portland. I thought about hanging on and sailing ashore but I soon realised that the 'chute was taking me the wrong way. I managed to release it and started to swim to the beach, about a quarter of a mile away. My arm was beginning to hurt and the left half of my Mae West had been punctured by the bullet so I floated a bit 'left wing low'. I had already taken off my boots and considered that losing my trousers would ease the situation a bit. As they floated away I suddenly remembered my fiver in the pocket! I couldn't quite reach them and I often wondered if anyone ever found my £5.''

Eventually Pilot Officer John Cock reached Chesil Beach to be greeted by some Home Guards armed with shot guns. 87 Squadron's Operational Record Book records the event thus . . . ''he arrived dressed in a tunic and blue underpants — a somewhat fearsome spectacle.''

Not all of 'B' Flight were so lucky. the Flight Commander, Flight Lieutenant Jeff DFC, did not return. He was last seen in a vertical dive off Portland Harbour.

Bob Payne had been watching the dog fights from the upper window of his cottage at Langton Herring. A Hurricane, trailing smoke, appeared in a shallow dive from the direction of Portland. It struck the water of the Fleet and

disappeared in a flurry of spray, leaving only a few pieces floating on the surface.

13 August was 'Alder Tag', Eagle Day, the day on which Göring had decreed the destruction of Fighter Command would begin. The great day, however, began disastrously for the Luftwaffe when operations were postponed only after some bomber units were beyond recall. At around 06.35 hours, the three Hurricanes of 'B' Flight were among the fighter units who engaged the Ju 88s of KG54 targeted to airfields including Middle Wallop and Andover. Squadron Leader 'Johnny' Dewar shot down a Ju 88 from which he watched one man bale out before it crashed into the sea. Pilot Officer Jay also brought down a Ju 88, in the Bognor area, which once more crashed into the sea. As the pilots reformed for the flight back to Exeter, Jay noticed white vapour coming from the engine of 'Dicky' Glyde's Hurricane, presumably as a result of damage substained in combat with the Ju 88s. Before Jay and Dewar could make a closer inspection, Glyde's Hurricane had vanished and a search of the area revealed nothing. 'Dicky' Glyde remains posted as missing and is presumed to have crashed, unobserved, into the sea.

The afternoon of 'Alder Tag' was a more organised affair with large formations of aircraft attacking airfields in southern England. Green Section, lead by Dennis David, were among the fighters that met a large, mixed force of Ju

Roland 'Bea' Beamont snapped as he returned smiling from a sortie during the Battle of Britain. Note the narrow outer yellow ring on the roundel and patching and repainting of the fabric aft of the cockpit.

87s, Ju 88s, Me 109s and Me 110s approaching the Dorset Coast. David lead his section sun-up and above the enemy before diving on them, each pilot chosing his target as they flashed past. David fired at a Ju 88 which was bombing Portland and, after a two second burst, he reported that the bomber followed his bombs down into the harbour.

Pilot Officer Mitchell, with 'B' Flight, attacked a formation of Me 110s and Ju 88s five miles south of Portland on the 14th. He claimed to have brought down one of the Me 110s and submitted a 'possible' claim for a Ju 88.

15 August could well be regarded as the climax of the Battle of Britain, for on that day the Luftwaffe made 1,786 sorties against targets which stretched along the east and south coasts from Northumberland to Cornwall. As usual, action over the west came after that in the south-east and did not begin until the afternoon. Once again, the Royal Naval dockyards were the intended target for the bombers that approached Portland. An estimated forty Ju 87s from I/StG 1 and 11/StG 2 were to make the attack, escorted by 20 Me 110s of V/LG2 and some 60 Me 109s form various Gruppen of JG 27 and JG 53. The fighter force which was sent against this was pitifully small in comparison; Nos 87 and 213 Squadrons from Exeter to tackle the Stukas and Me 110s, with the Spitfires of No 234 Squadron to occupy the fighter escort.

No 87 Squadron, lead by Squadron Leader Lovell-Gregg, took off in company with No 213 Squadron at 17.30 hours and climbed to around 15,000 feet over Portland. Lovell-Gregg had never been in combat before but was about to take part in what was described as "the fiercest dog fight yet experienced". The squadron had the advantage of height over the enemy and manoeuvred up-sun of the formation which stretched out below them. 'Widge' Gleed of 'A' Flight was one of the first to attack.

"On sighting enemy I lead flight in climb towards the sun, I dived unseen by EA out of the sun, attacked a Me 110 which burst into flames, broke away from flight climbed above and dived for vertical attack on Me 110, starboard engine of EA caught fire and broke from formation. Climbed up again and started chasing main formation towards France, in company with two Me 109s (I thought they were Hurricanes). They turned on me, one did a head on attack the other made for my tail, I got a good burst in on engine and undersurface of EA attacking head on. I then aileron-turned vertical downwards, one EA went down parallel, and the other tried to get on my tail, I pulled out and dived into cloud at 4,000 feet."

Following Gleed was Ken Tait, who first attacked an Me 110 which rolled onto its back and dived from 15,000 feet to 7,000 feet with the Hurricane following. After a final burst, Tait reported seeing the machine dive into the sea. Flying Officer Ward reported that the Me 110 he attacked rolled onto its back and dived vertically down. Flying Officer Rayner attacked some Me 110s which had formed a defensive circle and was himself attacked by three of them, one of which he claimed to have shot down into the sea.

Dennis David lead Green Section of 'B' Flight down onto some Stukas which were in their bombing dive and caused one to "follow his bombs into the sea one mile east of Portland Bill" before he became involved with the defending fighters. 'Bea' Beamont was about to attack a Stuka, when — "An Me 110 stall turned in front of me and I was able to fire a long burst into it at close range. After avoiding collision with it I saw it catch fire and dive, inverted into the sea."

Also from 'B' Flight, Pilot Officer Jay attacked an Me 110 but was forced to break away as fighters attacked him. He later reported: "A Ju 87 crossed my sights, I fired and the pilot baled out, I attacked a second Ju 87 which blew up and caught fire. I was then attacked by Me 110s and dived

Peter Comeley and 'Widge' Gleed relax in the summer sunshine between sorties, early August, 1940.

into cloud to escape, I climbed up again and ran into five Me 109s which attacked me, I concentrated on one and he went down with black smoke coming out. I then finished my ammunition and was shot down by the other Me 109s."

When, later that evening, stock could be taken and reports gathered together it was realised that 13 enemy aircraft had been claimed as destroyed. The claims were:

Flight Lieutenant Gleed	— Two Me 110s destroyed and one Me 109 probably destroyed.
Flight Officer Rayner	— One Me 110 destroyed and three damaged.
Pilot Officer Mitchell	— One Ju 87 and one Me 110 destroyed and one Me 110 damaged.
Pilot Officer Beamont	— One Me 110 destroyed and one probably destroyed.

Squadron Leader Terence Gunion Lovell-Gregg, was born in New Zealand in 1912 and died in Dorset, on August 15, 1940, in his first engagement (RAF Museum).

Flying Officer Ward	–	One Me 110 destroyed.
Flying Officer Tait	–	One Me 110 destroyed.
Pilot Office Jay	–	Two Ju 87s and one Me 109 destroyed.
Pilot Officer Comeley	–	One Me 110 destroyed.
Sergeant Cowley	–	One Me 110 destroyed and another probably destroyed.

Any feeling of triumph was, however, tempered by the losses the squadron had sustained. Pilot Officer Comeley's claim was reported by his fellow pilots as he was subsequently brought down by another Me 110 and crashed into the sea. Sergeant Cowley was returning to Exeter when the engine of his Hurricane failed and forced him to make a landing near Symonsbury. Cowley was slightly injured and transported to Bridport Hospital whilst his aircraft was later repaired. Pilot Officer Jay was also in trouble and headed for the nearest land, which turned out to be Weymouth. A resident saw the smoking Hurricane roar across the railway station and land in a field near Caffey's Lake, where the South African pilot got out with a broad grin and said "I've bagged three!" Before leaving the scene, Jay wrenched a panel with a painting of Lucifer and the name Diabolo on it from the fuselage. He explained that the painting had been on two other machines which he had crashed and emerged from unscathed. "I want it on my next one" he said.

Squadron Leader Lovell-Gregg also failed to return to Exeter from this, his first combat. Whether through inexperience or bad luck, his Hurricane was set on fire and he tried to regain the land which he crossed near Abbotsbury. As he circled the area losing height all the while Mr Durnford, a farmer, and his son watched the Hurricane as it eventually skimmed across a wood, landed in a ploughed field and carried on into a small copse where a wing struck an oak tree and broke up. When the Durnfords reached the burning wreck they found that the Squadron Leader's body had been thrown clear but that he was dead. He had wounds in his arms and legs and the upper part of his clothes were smouldering. When soldiers arrived they covered the body with his parachute and put it on a length of corrugated iron to carry to a waiting lorry. Later in the week, Ian Gleed, Derek Ward and Ken Tait flew from Exeter to attend the funeral of Terence Lovell-Gregg in the churchyard of the Holy Trinity Church at Warmwell. They were the only mourners.

For the next few days the squadron was not involved in aerial combat, though patrols were flown continuously. The focus of the Luftwaffe's activities shifted eastwards, where fierce combats took place in No Group's airspace of Sussex and Kent.

25 August saw the return of the Luftwaffe to the south west when, in the afternoon, a force of 45 Ju 88s escorted by over 200 fighters was detected assembling over Cherbourg. This formation consisted of Ju 88s form II/KG 51 and II/KG 54, Me 110s form I/ZG 2, II/ZG 2 and V/LG 1 with Me 109s form JG 53. With little else to occupy them, Fighter Command ordered 10 and 11 Groups to scramble squadrons from Exeter, Warmwell, Middle Wallop, Tangmere and Westhampnett.

As the enemy reached the coast near Weymouth Bay, the 13 Hurricanes of No 87 Squadron were the first fighters to make contact. Wing Commander Dewar led the squadron with 'B' Flight covered by 'A' Flight.

Flight Lieutenant Gleed wrote an account of this day in his wartime book *Arise to Conquer*, which captures the atmoshere of the day in a unique style. Gleed has just been told that the German invasion has begun:

"Damn the 'phone! 'Hullo! Yes, Ken, (Flying Officer Tait) is it today? Where? OK. Well, I'm retiring to readiness. I suppose we'll have to have a staggered lunch. Look after things, Adj; give me a ring if anything interesting comes in. I'll slip up at lunch-time to sign any bumf. I'm just going to Johnny's (Wing Commander Dewar's) office, then out to dispersal.' – 'Good luck, sir.' – 'Thanks.'

I knock. 'Come in. Good morning, Widge. Heard the news? Today is meant to be the great day.'

'Yes, I heard from Opps, sir. I wonder where on earth they are meant to be coming. Do you think they'll try it, sir?'

'No, Widge, but I think there will be another big blitz today, so I'm coming to fly with you.'

'That's grand, sir. Will you take your old place and lead the Squadron with 'B' Flight? I'll look after your tails with 'A' Flight.'

'Ok, Widge. Tell the 'B' Flight boys I'll be out in half an hour.'

'OK, sir; that will be about eleven.'

I bump across the 'drome, stop at 'B' Flight and tell Derek (Pilot Officer David) what is happening. Them bump across to 'A' Flight.

'Is "A" serviceable?'

'Yes, sir, it's all OK. Are you flying today?'

'I sincerely hope so. The invasion is meant to be starting today.'

'It's a grand day for it, anyway, sir.'

Wing Commander John Scatliff Dewar DSO, DFC, was born in India in 1907 and at the age of 33 was the highest ranking officer killed in the Battle of Britain.

Sergeant Cowley photographed by 'Watty' alongside his aircraft. He is holding his helmet and mask, with parachute and Mae West on the tail ready to don.

Jay walks through Weymouth after crash landing his Hurricane as described above (Hood via Clare).

It was: a cloudless blue sky. The boys were lying out on their beds in their shirt-sleeves. – 'Good morning, sir. Sleep well?' That was a crack from Robbie (Flying Officer Rayner) because I had overslept that morning.

'Good morning, Robbie. Very well, thank you. Have you heard the gen? Today is invasion day, and they are expecting a hell of a blitz. Johnny is going to lead us from ''B'' Flight. We are going to fix the escort fighters. Dickie and Dinkie Powell, (Sergeant Howell) you will be Red section with me. Who have you got, Robbie?'

'I'll take Watty and Vines' (Sergeant Wakeling).

'OK I bet you nothing happens at all, but still, here we are. Watty, have you got any models ready to fly? You make them and I'll break them.'

'I've built you a special one, sir; it's a super acrobatic model.'

Watty produces a beautifully made little model powered with many strands of elastic.

'Thank you very much, Watty; do you think I'm getting fat or something?'

'No, sir, but I don't want you to break my big 'planes.'

'OK, Watty; I trust that you will maintain this for me, anyway. Come on, Dinkie; you hold it and I'll wind.'

We wind the elastic up with a drill; steady the elevators.

'OK. Well, here goes. Christ, what a climb!'

The model whips into the air, soars up to about 100 feet, rolls on its back, loops, then climbs in a tight circle. The elastic unwinds and the prop starts free-wheeling; it settles into a steady glide and touches down and lands on its wheels. A minute and a half. 'Damn good, Watty.' I have a couple of hundred yards' walk to collect it.

We sit about. I lie on a bed and write letters, one to Pam, another to my mother, and yet another to the Upper Thames Sailing Club asking them about keeping my boat Spindrift there. The sun is very hot. Opps 'phone and tell me that 'A' Flight's job is to stop the escort fighters interfering with 'B' Flight and 213 Squadron, who have been ordered to deal with the bombers. All is quiet. The usual arguments ensue on who should go to lunch first. Robbie and I toss up, and he loses. So once more Red section goes first, with lots of moans from Watty and Vines (the new pilot), who swear that I must have a double-sided coin (unfortunately not true).

'Come on, Dickie; we haven't got all day. I suppose Vines will be all right.' – 'Oh, I think so, sir; he has done a lot of patrols now, but hasn't seen any Jerries.' – 'How much time has he done on ''Hurries''?' – 'About fifty hours now.' – 'Well, that should be plenty. If he survives his first blitz I think he'll be a good pilot. He's very steady.'

We swallow our lunch and rocket out to dispersal. 'Hold on a second. I must just rush upstairs and see if there is any bumf to sign. Shan't be a second. – Hullo, Adj! Everything under control?'

'Please sign these two files, sir; then everything is under control.'

'Are you ready for the invasion, Adj? Have you got your revolver? – Good Show! Well, keep the Hun out of the office while you burn the files.'

'OK, sir. I'll have a large beer for you when you are released.'

'OK, Adj; that's a date. I must rush off now. Keep everything under control, and ring me if anything interesting comes in.'

'Right; off we go.'

'Have you fixed it that we get lots of tea, Dickie?'

'Yes, Widge, it is all fixed.'

'Good!'

Back to readiness to have a siesta on our beds. All is quiet. Everything seems very peaceful. The afternoon drifts

Sgt Cowley, 'Rubber' Thorogood and Roddy Rayner at Exeter with personal transport between sorties (Watson).

slowly by. My thoughts are far away sailing on blue seas with Pamela.

'I wonder if it will be a blitz like last time, Robbie?'

'I hope not, old boy; it was too hot for comfort.'

'I should like about 20 Junker 87s to appear with no escort.'

'That would just about suit me too.'

'Actually, Robbie, what do you think the best way of attacking those really big formations is?'

'I don't know, Widge. The only thing that I am certain of is that the 109s are miles above the 110s, ready to pounce on anything that attacks them, and the 110s in their turn pounce on anything that makes a dart at the bombers. In fact, the whole thing is damned unpleasant. We can't possibly get above those 109s – they're floating about at thirty thousand. The only thing to do is to try to get them mixed up, then nibble at the edges. Don't let's think about it, Widge; I'm going to sleep. Wake me when the tea comes, before you have ganneted it all.'

'Happy dreams, Robbie.'

We lie about. The birds fly. Watty brings out his new model, gives it many winds; it soars upwards, catches a thermal up-current and nearly disappears from sight. It lands after a flight of eight minutes right the other side of the 'drome. Watty sends a van to fetch it. He is very pleased.

'Come on, Watty; hold my little devil.' We wind it up; it soars up, does two loops, a roll off the top, then a steady glide.

'It's wizard, Watty. Blast! it's going to crash on the haystack.'

It does. We get the ladder to fetch it down. I am half-way up

'Watty' and his models. The pilots are left to right, Thorogood, de Spirlet, Malengreau, Tait and 'Watty' Watson himself.

the ladder. Brrrrring . . . Hell! I jump off and run for the hut. The orderly is already at the 'phone.

'What is it?'

'Super readiness, boys.'

The boys drop their books and run to their 'planes.

'Flight, see that my men have everything ready for me in the cockpit. My parachute is out there. I'll stay by the 'phone.'

'Hullo, Opps. Squadron Leader Leeds (Gleed) here. How many are there this time? 150 plus . . . Whew! Hell's bells! Try to get us off in plenty of time.'

'You'll be off soon.'

I peer out of the window. The boys are already in the cockpits — 'Hullo, Opps! ''A'' Flight now at super readiness. Thanks a lot.'

I sit on the bed, idly turning over the pages of one of Watty's model aeroplane magazines. My mouth is dry. God! why must there be wars? I wonder if all the boys feel as frightened as I do. They at least don't know that a hundred and fifty plus is on the way. Suppose the two Squadrons from Warmwell go up with 213 Squadron and ourselves, it will be at the most 48 planes, probably 36. How the hell can we stop them? I wonder what the Jerries feel like, flying in their huge formations. I untwist the cock on my Mae West and give it a couple of puffs; it's working all right, anyway. Brrrrring. Oh God, here it is! Patrol Portland. 'START UP!' I scream. 'You are to fix escort fighters.' 'Phone down, I run like hell, bound towards 'A'. The engine starts. Good boys! Dixon, the fitter, is out of the cockpit like a flash and holds my parachute ready for me to slip in. I clamber up the wing and drop in the cockpit. He puts the straps on my shoulders; I fix the safety-pin.

'Good hunting, sir.'

'Thanks.'

He jumps off the wing. I open the throttle and start taxiing. 'B' Flight boys are roaring off the ground — three, four, five. I have picked my helmet off my reflector sight and have buckled my chinstrap just as 'B' Flight's sixth 'plane is off. Throttle open and we are off. A quick glance behind shows the others taking off in quick succession. I throttle back a bit to give Dickie and Dinkie a chance to get into position. Johnny, the Station Commander, is leading us on a straight course for Portland. Hold hard, Johnny: we'll never catch you at this rate. In my mirror I can see Robbie's boys just catching us up; we are climbing hard.

'Crocodile calling Suncup leader. Are you receiving me?' — 'Suncup leader answering. Loud and clear.' — 'Crocodile receiving Suncup loud and clear.' — 'Listen out.' 'Crocodile calling Bearskin leader. Are you

Gleed lands 'A' at Hullavington in late 1940, in a scene repeated many times in that eventful year.

receiving?' — Faintly I hear, 'Receiving you loud and clear.'

I glance back at the 'drome. Twelve dots are climbing behind us. Lucky devils, 213 Squadron: they are after the bombers again. It's a glorious day. The sun beats down on us. The sea looks most inviting. Hope I don't have a bathe just yet. At last we are slowly catching ''B'' Flight up. I glance at the instrument panel. Everything looks normal: radiator temperature on the high side, nothing to worry about, as it's a hell of a hot day. It seems hard to realise that over the sea masses of Jerry aircraft are flying, aiming to drop their bombs on the peaceful-looking countryside that lies beneath. Up, up. My two wing men are crouching forward in their cockpits, their hoods open. I slide mine open: it's too damned stuffy with it shut. My mouth feels hellishly dry; there is a strong sinking feeling in my breast. Thank God a doctor isn't listening to my heart. It's absolutely banging away. Turn on the oxygen a bit more. We are now at 20,000. It is cooler now, so I slam the hood shut. It's a hell of a long way to fall. Once more the sun shines from the sea; its reflection off the surface makes it nearly impossible to look in that direction. Yet that direction is where the Hun is coming from. At last, 25,000 feet. We all throttle back and close up. I climb to 26,000, level out. On the RT rather faintly comes, 'Bandits now south-west of Portland Bill.' We are in perfect position to intercept them.

Below us, like a model, lies Portland harbour. A sunken ship standing in shallow waters, half submerged, looks like a microscopic model. Back with the hood. I strain my eyes peering at the blue sky. Nothing yet. Far below us another squadron is weaving; just below me 'B' Flight is weaving violently. Dickie and Dinkie criss-cross behind my tail. I peer forwards, heading out to sea.

'Tally-ho.' 'Christ! there they are.' A weaving, darting mass of dots gradually drift towards us, looking like a cloud of midges on a summer evening. 'Hell! was I born to die today?'

'Line astern, line astern, go.'

Dickie and Dinkie swing under my tail. The Jerries seem miles above us; lines of smaller dots show where the 109s are ready to pounce. Beneath them, about our height, circles of 110s turn, chasing each others' tails, moving as a mass slowly towards us. Far below, the bombers are in tight formation. Somehow they look like tin soldiers. 'Steady; don't attack too soon.' Johnny and 'B' Flight have dived, heading for the bombers; they have swung into line astern and now swing into echelon. The 110s continue circling. They seem to make no attempt to dive.

'Here goes.'

I dive at the nearest circle of 110s.

'Christ! look out.'

A model aeroplane enthusiast all his life, 'Watty' Watson, who died in 1986, passed his interest to his grandson, Nicholas.

A glance behind shows 109s literally falling out of the sky, on top of us. Messerschmitts. I bank into a steep turn. Now we are in a defensive circle, the 109s overshoot us and climb steeply. Now's our chance. I straighten out and go for the closest 110. 'You silly b———!' He turns away from me. I turn the firing-button on to fire; at exactly 250 yards I give him a quick burst. White puffs are flashing past the cockpit. Another burst. Got him! A terrific burst of fire from his starboard engine, a black dot and a puff of white as the pilot's parachute opens. I bank into a steep left-hand turn and watch for a split second the burning 110 going vertically downwards. The parachutist is surrounded by 'planes, darting here and there. 'Thank God! got one of them. Now for another.' Below me another circle of nine 110s are firing at a solitary Hurricane which is turning inside them. I shove the nose down, sights on the last one, thumb the firing-button. 'Oh, what a lovely deflection shot! Got him!' White smoke pours from one engine, more white vapour from his wings; his wings glint as he rolls on his back. Another burst. Hell, look out! A large chunk of something flashes by my wings; as I glance behind I see tracer flash by my tail.

A 109 is just about on my tail; the stick comes back in my tummy, and everything goes away. Now an aileron turn downwards, down. 'Hell! that was a near one.' I miss a 110 by inches – down; at 400 mph on the clock. The controls are solid. Nothing seems to be behind me. I wind gently on the trimming wheel, straighten out and start a steep climb. What seems miles above me the Jerries still whirl. I can't see any friendly 'planes at all. 'Hell! where am I? About 10 miles off the coast. Hurrah! they're going home.' I turn for the shore, weaving fiercely. 'Hell! over to the west the bombers are haring back in twos and threes.' Two Hurricanes appear to be chasing them. I can catch them easily. 'Here goes. There's one. Looks like an 88. That will do me nicely.' The escort fighters still seem a long way above me. I am gaining fast – about 400 yards now. 'Hell! . . . the Hurricanes have black crosses on them – 109s; coming straight for me, head-on attack. Right, you bastards! I'll give you hell before you get me.' Sights on, I thumb the button. A stream of tracer tears over my head. 'Blast! missed him. Now come on, number two.' He heads straight

for me. I yank back on the stick, kick on rudder and turn down on to the 109. 'That shook you up, didn't it?' Sights on. Brmmmmmm, brrrrrrrmmmmm. A streak of black comes from his engine, a stream of tracer flashes past my nose. 'God, I must get out of this.' Another aileron turn. 'Down, down, down. Pull out now, or you'll be in "the drink".' The coast is nearly out of sight. 'Oh God, don't let them get me.' I screw round in the cockpit. Nothing is in sight. I scream along just above the water. I glance at the rev counter. I'm so deaf that I'm not at all sure that the motor is going. It looks all right. I hurtle past many patches of oil. At last the cliffs loom up. I turn westwards. Several patches of fluorescence show where pilots are in the water. Motor-boats are chugging towards them. The sea is dead calm, glassy.

'I'm still alive.'

I skim past a tyre, many patches of oil. – 'Poor devil! wonder what that was off?' I wonder if all the boys are OK. These damned Jerries don't press very hard. I bet they are feeling sore. Sidmouth looks lovely as I roar low over the coast.

'Whew! I could do with a bathe.'

People in the water look up and wave. I wave back and give them a thumbs up. 'Good old "A"! here we are at last.' I roar low over our dispersal hut. All of 'B' Flight appear to be down. Round the circuit and swiftly into land.

I bump across the 'drome into the dispersal position; then men run out to meet me.

'How many, sir?' I put two fingers up. 'And I damaged another'.

'How many of the boys are back?' – 'All but one now, sir. Sergeant Vines is still up. All of 'B' Flight are down. Every pilot seems to have got at least one.'

'That's grand. Have a good look for bullet-holes. I don't think there are any, but you never know.'

'Did you pull the tit, sir?'

'No, not this time.'

'Hullo, Ken! how are we doing?'

'Very well, sir. "B" Flight have got six confirmed and three probables. What did you get?'

'Two 110s confirmed and a 109 damaged.'

'Bea' Beamont, photographed by 'Watty', in summer 1940 was one of the squadron's most successful pilots and, of course, went on to a long and successful career both in the RAF and as a test pilot.

Johnny Cock was recovering at Babbacombe when the telegram informing James Nicholson that he had been awarded the Victoria Cross arrived. They are seen shaking hands, whilst other pilots look on. A strange coincidence occured in April 1983 when John returned to England to witness the recovery of his Hurricane the very weekend that Nicholson's VC was auctioned at Sothebys.

'Damn good show, sir!'

'Hullo, Watty! How did you get on?'

'I didn't, sir. Nine 109s seemed to think I was their pet Hurricane; they fought me for about 20 minutes till I thought my arm would fall off. I only managed to get one burst in. I definitely hit one of the b————s, though I'm damned if I know what happened to him. Anyway, eight of the b————s still chased me. Honestly, old boy, I thought they'd get me. There was a hell of a bang once; the crew have managed to find five bullet-holes in the tail-'plane. How did you get on, Widge?'

'Very fine to start with. I suppose you saw my flamer? It most certainly lit the sky up. Did you see the pilot bale out? God! I bet he was petrified. 'Planes were whistling by him. If I had baled out I should have done a delayed drop. Who the hell was surrounded by 110s just after we had attacked?'

'That was me, Widge,' Dickie said. 'I suppose it was you who butted in. Many thanks. I saw you hit somebody's glycol tank. God knows what happened to it. I got one of them – went in with a hell of a splash, then the 109s descended. I had a hell of a fight with them. They most certainly wasted a lot of ammo. For about five minutes solid tracer appeared to be just missing the windscreen. I smacked one of them in flames; after doing about 100 steep turns, the other b————s went away.'

Robbie said, 'I've got one bullet thorough the wing-tip that hasn't done any damage at all. I say, Widge, where do you think Vines is? Did anybody see him after we had attacked? I think he turned to meet those first 109s. I didn't see him after that. I fired my guns at Heaven knows how many Jerries, but only saw one go for a burton; his wings fell off about 5,000 feet beneath me. It gave me a hell of a shock. Did you see that one that crashed on the beach? There was a hell of an explosion when it hit. It must have been a bomber. Every time I looked down there was another patch of oil. Thank God they turned back when they did, otherwise I think we should have all been swimming about the ''drink''. My arm just about dropped off.'

'I hope Vines is OK I'll 'phone Opps and see if they have got any dope on the crashes. – Hullo, Opps. CO 87 here. Have you any dope on our crashes? We are still minus Sergeant Vines – OK; give me a ring as soon as you hear anything. – Opps don't know a thing. There has been a hell of a blitz all along the coast. They made a dash at London, but turned back. Already there are well over 100 combats in Fighter Command.'

'Telephone for you, sir.' – 'Hullo, Billie. – It's 213. – How did you get on? Hey, I said it first. Come on, Billie, what's the dope? – Ten confirmed and seven probables? Damned good! Who's missing? – Two Belgians? I'm damned sorry; I hope they'll be all right. We got nine confirmed and four probables. One missing – Sergeant Vines. Mostly fighters. No, you didn't get 87 dive-bombers again? You lucky devils! We had the damned escort fighters to fix. See you in the bar.'

'They are lucky devils – they had the dive-bombers again. They have lost their two Belgians. Do you remember after the last show, when Matters asked one of them how many he attacked, he answered, ''Me, I attack no one. I defence myself''.'

He had shot down three. Now he was missing.

We sat around. The evening was incredibly still, the hills behind the 'drome turned purple, the sun sank. The day blitz seemed like some fantastic dream. The corn in the fields looked a glorious yellow. It was very wonderful just being alive. Watty got his models out and we chased them across the 'drome. It got cooler. We retired to our hut and put our uniforms on.

'Opps, any news of anyone? – No. Hell! Well, what

Late summer, 1940. Left to right: 'Watty' Watson, 'Rubber' Thorogood, Roger Malengreau, 'Widge' Gleed, Ken Tait and Roddy Rayner (Watson).

about getting us released?' – 'OK. Just hang on and we'll bind Group.'

'Damn good show on your boy's part today. We are all very proud of you.'

'Hullo! Group send their heartiest congrats to 87, and say you are released till 05.30. Hold on a second, Widge. Who's doing the early morning readiness?'

'I regret to say 'A' Flight.'

'OK. See you shortly. You like lager, don't you?'

'Thanks awfully; yes, please, Opps.'

We pushed off to the bar. There was the usual terrific crowd and jumbled conversation. Once more the colours of the different bottles and the healthy tan of the pilot's faces seemed to be more vivid than usual. My heart seemed free. Things gradually became happily bleary as we drank each other's health. At last the party was over. We staggered out to the car; the air smelt delicious. A bumpy ride across the 'drome and we fell into the dispersal hut, rather unsteadily clambered into bed, after carefully folding our clothes, ready to put on over our pyjamas in the morning. 'Last in bed puts the light out.' There was a hell of a scurry to put our pyjamas on. Dickie was last, as usual. So he had to blow the hurricane lamp out. Mighty curses as he bashed his legs on his camp bed as he clambered in. All was silent. Robbie was quietly puffing at a cigarette. 'Well, boys, I'm afraid that Vines has had it. I'll have to write to his people tomorrow. Thanks for a grand performance today. Happy dreams.' – 'Good night, Widge, sir. Happy dreams to you.'

The hut was silent now, except for muffled conversation from the men's section behind a thin wooden partition. I turned on my side and shut my eyes. Once again death had been very near to me. 'Pray God that they don't come to-morrow; that would be too much. I must buy a sleeping-bag.' Before I slept, pictures of my sailing-boat floated before my eyes. I saw Pam laughing as I got a wave over me as we launched her. I fell asleep.

Wing Commander 'Johnny' Dewar wrote the following report which gives a less emotive and more formal version of the events.

''Led squadron to patrol Warmwell at 10,000 feet as ordered. Sighted AA bursts over Portland but no aircraft. Then sighted large enemy force coming westwards along coast. Selected squadron of Ju 88s least escorted and led in on a gentle quarter attack. Fired about 800 rounds, as I pulled away I saw aircraft smoking. F/Sgt Badger who was following saw it burst into flames. It must have fallen near

35

Sergeant Wakeling with teachers from Latimer Grammar School shortly after winning his wings. He was 'bounced' by Me 109s over Dorset on August 25, during his first combat, locals believe they saw him being shot at whilst hanging from his parachute.

Lulworth. Later it was confirmed by Observer Corps that one fell there. I continued my turn on pulling away and met around 10 Me 110s head on taking a fleeting burst at one. By the time I had turned around again I could see no aircraft near me. Beyond Lulworth there was a huge circle of wheeling aircraft. Every now and then one dropped out smoking. The bombers seemed to be making out to sea. Very high over Portland way a white Very light was fired. I flew climbing towards the west, turning now and again to sweep the sky above. During one of these turns I almost collided with an Me 109 turning in the opposite direction. I started to persue as he went past me and saw that he was the leader of four. They did not seem to have seen me so I joined them — in the rear. Unfortunately their initial speed did not allow me to get nearer than about 600 yards and although I had +9 on the boost I could not catch up. As they turned, however, I slowly gained. When about 300 yards away I opened fire on the rearmost in short bursts. He immediately turned more steeply than the rest and increased speed, but not before vapour came pouring from him. His manoeuvre carried him to the front of the others and I had to break off action with him. Last seen he was diving at about 45 degrees slightly banked and may have come down near Lulworth also on the Cove or in the sea. Fumes were pouring from him. I suspect he carried armour as I fired at least 800 rounds with almost dead astern shots. The others climbed quickly out of reach.''

As the fight sprawled over the Dorset Coast, the other pilots all had opportunity to make attacks and subsequently file combat reports. It is particularly plain in this case that the claims far out-numbered the total enemy aircraft lost, particularly when it is remembered that other squadrons were also involved. Nevertheless, the reports were submitted in good faith and must be regarded as such.

Ken Tait brought down an Me 110 into the sea and then attacked an Me 109 which he followed down until it crashed and exploded on Chesil Bank. There is little doubt that this machine crashed, nor is there any doubt about the Me 109 which 'Bea' Beamont recalls attacking.

''I was just behind an Me 109 at about 8,000 feet, with my thumb on the gun button waiting for him to stop weaving about. I managed to get a long burst into the 109 and he dropped to about 700 feet. I followed him down waiting to see if he was going to land or suddenly dart off to sea. He suddenly did a barrel-roll, possibly to throw off my aim and then went into a steep side slipping left turn down and made a very competent belly landing in a small field. I flew down low over the 109 and saw the pilot get out, and I thought — this is when the Germans are supposed to strafe the pilots on the ground! But it didn't seem a good idea to me so I flew round again and opened the cockpit hood and waved at him. He waved back and I then saw the 109 burst into flames; the aircraft was smoking when it was landing. A few days later the Army brought a fine Luger pistol and holster to me at Exeter, with the 109 pilot's compliments.''

The total claims list compiled for the squadron's Operational Record Book features:

Wing Commander Dewar	— One Ju 88 destroyed and one Me 109 probably destroyed.
Flight Lieutenant Gleed	— One Me 110 destroyed and another probably destroyed, one Me 109 damaged.
Pilot Officer David	— One Ju 88 and one Me 109 destroyed.
Pilot Officer Mitchell	— One Me 109 destroyed.
Pilot Officer Beamont	— One Me 109 destroyed and one Do 17 probably destroyed.
Flying Officer Tait	— One Me 110 and one Me 109 destroyed.
Flying Officer Watson	— One Me 109 damaged.
Flight Sergeant Badger	— One Ju 88 probably destroyed and one Me 109 damaged.
Pilot Officer Malengreau	— One Ju 88 damaged.
Sergeant Howell	— One Me 109 probably destroyed.
Sergeant Thorogood	— One Ju 88 destroyed.

The squadron's only loss was, as Gleed noted, Sergeant Wakeling. 'Stump' as his fellow pilots called him, was shot

Warmwell cemetery, where both Lovell-Gregg and Wakeling lie.

down when Me 109s of JG 53 first attacked 'B' Flight and his Hurricane was seen to go down in a ball of flame over Dorchester. At the last moment he jumped clear but fell on a road-side only yards from his aircraft, with the silk of his unopened parachute flapping in the wind.

Again, a period of inactivity on the part of the Luftwaffe provided the squadron's pilots with time to reflect upon the events of the past weeks. The young men's emotions had swung through a range seldom experienced, save in time of war. There had been moments of great excitement, of terror, of grief and anticipation of what may happen with the coming of the next hour or day. Strain, both mental and physical could be discerned in the pilots, some of whom had been flying on operations for over a year.

Another long period of waiting and tension descended upon Exeter and the squadron. Continuous patrols became tedium when, day after day, the enemy failed to materialise.

On 3 September, the first anniversary of the war, orders came from 10 Group that 'B' Flight should move to Bibury to restart the night patrols. The weather was perfect and, on the first patrol, Pilot Officer Beamont saw a bomber coned in searchlights to the south east of Bristol. Anti aircraft fire was bursting around his target and the rear gunner seemed to be preoccupied with firing down the searchlight beams as Beamont manoeuvred for position. Suddenly, the bomber went into a steep dive, almost reaching the vertical as

Beamont opened fire. De Wilde incendiary and tracer ammunition struck the enemy's fuselage as both aircraft twisted in and out of the blinding beams of light. And then enemy had gone, lost to the night.

The following night, Beamont and Pilot Officer Jay again engaged a Ju 88 which they succeeded in damaging before it escaped in the darkness. Squadron Leader Dewar, now the Commanding Officer of Exeter, borrowed one of No 87 Squadron's Hurricanes to fly to Tangmere on 12 September. Although it was not intended to be an operational sortie, Dewar was informed of the presence of enemy aircraft in the area of Southampton. What happened to the Squadron Leader can only be conjecture as he never arrived at his destination, it is, however, believed that he was shot down and was forced to bale out into the sea from which his body was recovered eighteen days later.

News came, on 15 September, that Flight Lieutenant Ian 'Widge' Gleed had been awarded the DFC for his leadership of the squadron in some of their largest combats. Later on in the day, Dennis David and Pilot Officer Jay brought down an He 111 of Wetteredkundungs Staffel 51 which crashed into the sea off Bolt Head. Their engagement was, however, a tiny side show in comparison with the huge engagements which raged over south eastern England as London became the Luftwaffe's main target. 15 September has now become known as 'Battle of Britain Day'.

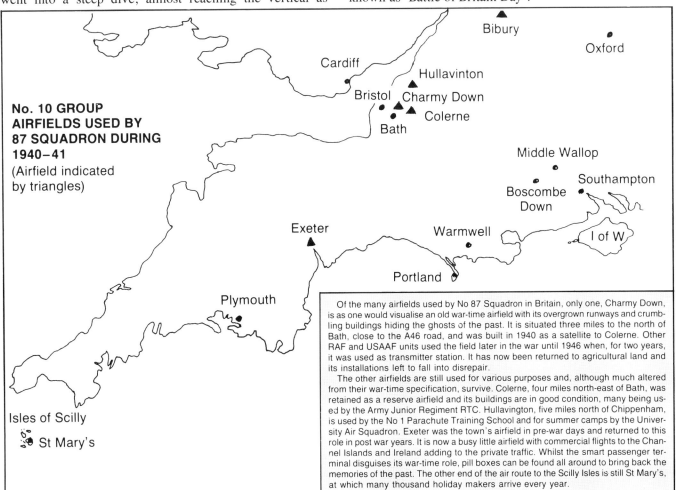

No. 10 GROUP AIRFIELDS USED BY 87 SQUADRON DURING 1940–41
(Airfield indicated by triangles)

Of the many airfields used by No 87 Squadron in Britain, only one, Charmy Down, is as one would visualise an old war-time airfield with its overgrown runways and crumbling buildings hiding the ghosts of the past. It is situated three miles to the north of Bath, close to the A46 road, and was built in 1940 as a satellite to Colerne. Other RAF and USAAF units used the field later in the war until 1946 when, for two years, it was used as transmitter station. It has now been returned to agricultural land and its installations left to fall into disrepair.

The other airfields are still used for various purposes and, although much altered from their war-time specification, survive. Colerne, four miles north-east of Bath, was retained as a reserve airfield and its buildings are in good condition, many being used by the Army Junior Regiment RTC. Hullavington, five miles north of Chippenham, is used by the No 1 Parachute Training School and for summer camps by the University Air Squadron. Exeter was the town's airfield in pre-war days and returned to this role in post war years. It is now a busy little airfield with commercial flights to the Channel Islands and Ireland adding to the private traffic. Whilst the smart passenger terminal disguises its war-time role, pill boxes can be found all around to bring back the memories of the past. The other end of the air route to the Scilly Isles is still St Mary's, at which many thousand holiday makers arrive every year.

Roland 'Bea' Beamont takes pains to stress that there is no 'u' in his name, as many seem to insist on inserting. After being awarded the DFC, 'Bea' left No 87 Squadron and flew for a short time with No 79 Squadron before becoming a test pilot for Hawker's where he tested Hurricanes and early Typhoons. With his experience, he was posted to No 56 Squadron as flight commander using the Typhoon operationally and continued this with No 609 Squadron, of which he became the commanding officer. At the end of his second tour he returned to Hawker's to test the Tempest and then introduced the machine with Nos 3, 486 and 56 Squadrons, as the wing leader. By October 1944, he had made 94 operational sorties over Europe and was offered a job with Hawker's. He refused this as he wanted to complete 100 sorties, but was shot down and taken prisoner on his very next flight. After being released by the Russians, he formed a Tempest wing which would have flown in the Far East, but the war came to an end and he became a test pilot for Gloucester's, flying Meteors. He then joined the English Electric Co as Chief Test Pilot and after a successful career in aviation retired in 1979 as a director of British Aerospace with special responsibility for the Panavia Tornado project.

Aside from 'Bea's' career in aviation, he was awarded the CBE in 1968 and appointed Deputy Lieutenant for Lancaster in 1977. He is now retired and lives in Hampshire with his wife Pat, who helps with charity work, lectures and tending the garden.

5. End of Battle

On 30 September, the weather improved in the south and south-east and, although there was still a good deal of cloud cover, the Luftwaffe took the opportunity to launch a series of attacks that forced Fighter Command into its heaviest day's activity of the month.

Operations had been taking place throughout the day over south-eastern England, but only in the afternoon did any significant activity take place in 10 Group's area. The opening gambit of these attacks came in the form of a feint attack by 12 aircraft against Southampton. As this force turned back over the Isle of Wight, an estimated fifty He 111s of the Stab, I and II Gruppen KG55 escorted by forty Me 110s from ZG 26 and fifty-two Me 109s of JGs 2 and 53, approached Portland; their task was to destroy the Westland aircraft factory at Yeovil. Against this raid, the following squadrons were scrambled: Nos 56, 609, 213, 607, 152 and 'B' Flight of No 87 Squadron.

Pilot Officers McLure and Johnny Cock, together with Sergeant Walton were the first of the squadron's pilots to take off and 'Widge' Gleed, who had come down from Bibury for the afternoon, followed. Three others had to refuel before they could take off and Flight Lieutenant Ward dashed from the cinema when he heard the sirens, but all were too late to meet the enemy.

At 16.35 hours, the first two pilots sighted the enemy flying above the 10/10 cloud cover which stretched over Portland and, manoeuvring so as to dive from out of the sun, dived on the formation. McLure was the first to attack:

"I dived down on the bombers and observed an Me 110 on my tail. I turned steeply in a left hand climbing turn and got on the 110s tail. I again turned steeply across the top and delivered my attack from about 200 yards. The starboard engine caught fire and it dived away through the clouds which were about 14,000 feet below. I again climbed up-sun and again attacked the other group of bombers — quarter attacks. The one aimed at seemed to go out of control and diverted slightly but resumed its course again. On my third burst it dived steeply, but I was unable to observe it further as my ammunition was exhausted and I had to outmanoeuvre several fighters that were on my tail."

Sergeant Walton followed the formation further inland but was shot down and forced to bale out of his Hurricane, which dived vertically into the ground on the outskirts of Sherbourne. Johnny Cock was attacked by an Me 109 which overshot him and enabled him to fire as it passed in front. The Me 109 slipped sideways into the cloud, with black smoke coming from it and Cock followed, but on emerging from the cloud he saw not the fighter but a bomber. After two brief attacks the starboard engine and fuselage caught fire and the bomber disappeared into cloud once more.

The final pilot to attack was 'Widge' Gleed, who found himself alone with a formation of 70 bombers, one of which he sent spiralling down before return fire hit his Hurricane and forced him to leave the area.

No 87 Squadron, together with the other squadrons, successfully prevented the attack destroying its target and not a single bomb fell on the Westland factory.

The engagement of 30 September was the last large scale action that the squadron was to become involved in for, on 1 October, the squadron was ordered to move to Colerne to take part in night patrols on a permanant basis.

Whilst the large scale actions for which the 'Battle of Britain' is best known continued on occasion over south eastern England, only rarely did an enemy machine venture over the West Country. One of the most successful of the squadron's pilots, Pilot Officer 'Bea' Beamont, intercepted four Me 110s in daylight over Portland on 11 October. After a head-on attack, the leader of the enemy formation dived vertically into cloud and was lost to sight, Beamont could only submit a claim for an enemy aircraft damaged.

Trevor Jay, whose luck finally ran out in the flying accident of October 24, 1940.

The tail of John Cock's Hurricane after the collision with Jay's aircraft that led to the unfortunate death of Jay.

Sergeant Alex Thom, posted to the squadron October 30, 1940.

'Watty' Watson examines the control column excavated from Sergeant Walton's Hurricane, 44 years to the day after it crashed (Congram).

One of the last entries to be made in the squadron's Operational Record Book for the 'Battle of Britain' was made on 29 October. It recorded the burial of Pilot Officer Jay, who had been killed in a tragic accident five days previously whilst returning from patrol in a 'box of four' formation. Ahead of Jay, was Johnny Cock, who was leading the flight when he began to experience difficulties with his Hurricane's fuel supply, the Merlin engine faltered and Jay's Hurricane ran into the tail of Cock's machine. Johnny Cock, regained control after the collision and made a perfect landing at Exeter but, with his propeller blades shattered, Jay had no alternative but to bale out, despite being at only 1,800 feet above Lyme Bay. He was seen to climb out into the port wing and wave to his colleagues

before he jumped, but as the slipstream whisked him backwards he hit the tail plane and was, presumably, knocked unconscious. Beamont and Mitchell, the other two pilots in the formation, could do nothing but look on as Jay's body fell to earth and landed on top of a 1,000 feet high hill near Ashcoombe. The luckless pilot's body was rapidly recovered and he lived for an hour before succumbing to his injuries whilst en-route to hospital. This time, his fourth crash, lucky charms and gaily painted panels taken from previous machines could not save him.

This was the last of the squadron's casualties in the 'Battle of Britain', which totalled eight killed and five injured, with 15 machines being damaged or destroyed.

Divers raise the tail section of Johnny Cock's Hurricane which crashed in August 1940, from the waters of the Fleet.

Two weeks after the recovery, the author was able to present John with the gunsight from his Hurricane, at a dinner organised at the Victory Forces Club in London (Watson).

'Johnny' Cock was, and still is, the comedian of the squadron and an Australian through and through. John managed to come through the Battle of France unscathed and narrowly escaped death when brought down over Portland on August 11, 1940. After a tour as an instructor, he was posted No 453 Squadron as a flight commander and then to No 222 Squadron. He returned to Australia and, in May 1943, he was posted to No 54 Squadron, in the Pacific. In 1944 he returned to Britain and became the commanding officer of No 3 Squadron. After the war John settled in Queensland, where he and his wife Val ran a supermarket until their retirement and now spend much of their time working for charities and enjoying the Australian 'great outdoors'.

Recovery of what was thought to be 'Johnny' Cock's aircraft started on April 30, 1983, the Saturday of the May Bank Holiday weekend. A working platform was assembled and rowed out to the site by about twenty Royal Engineers apprentices who also provided a fourth assault craft to use as a ferry. That afternoon the recovery began, with six ex-87 Squadron pilots – John Cock, Dennis David, 'Dimmy' Joyce, 'Watty' Watson, Roland Beamont and Frank 'Dinkie' Howell with historian John Holloway all bobbing around on the raft. Pieces began to surface thick and fast. Notable amongst the finds was a badly bent panel bearing the number V7233, the first concrete evidence that this was John's plane.

A Hurricane 1 fitted with exhaust shield to prevent the pilot being dazzled by the flames during night operations.

6. Night Flying

Whatever the Air Ministry and Fighter Command may have said, the Hurricane was principally a day fighter which could be flown at night in relative safety by experienced pilots. It certainly was not an ideal night fighter, but necessity forced its use in an attempt to combat the increasing nocturnal activities of the Luftwaffe.

The squadron had already discovered how dangerous night operations could be when Sergeant Culverwell had been killed on 25 July and it says much for the skill of the pilots that there had been no more fatal accidents since. The pilots that flew these sorties recall how easy it was to become disorientated when relying upon the dim glimmer of the tiny cockpit lamp to illuminate the instruments. The occasional searchlight beam that could instantly dazzle one as if a light were switched on in a darkened room. Eyes screwed up tight against the blinding beam, yet straining to see either instruments or horizon. The myriad of stars and the moon above and flashes from shell bursts below with occasionally a fire glowing on the ground. Despite all this, a man was supposed to control his machine and find the enemy with nothing but his eyes and cryptic clues from the ground station to guide him.

Often the first indication of the presence of the enemy was the 'bump' as the Hurricane crossed turbulance left in the wake of a bomber and then the chase commenced. The pilot would pull the boost control to give maximum power to catch the enemy of which he hoped to catch a glimpse at any moment and then it appeared, as if out of nothing, a vague outline, stabbing exhaust flames. All feeling of the penetrating cold in the pilot's body turned to the warmth of excitement and fear as he throttled back to keep station behind his target. Tracer pours from the bomber's rearward firing gun and in return the Hurricane pilot fires his eight .303 inch Brownings. If his aim was accurate then flashes could be seen dancing along the body or wings of the enemy and

perhaps a fire would start in an engine. Invariably, this would all be accompanied by violent evasive action from the bomber's pilot in an effort to throw off his pursuer, little wonder then that few of No 87 Squadron's night sorties met with success.

Towards the end of 1940, some of the squadron's most experienced pilots were posted away. Dennis David, who had been with No 87 Squadron throughout the war and was its highest scoring pilot, left to join No 152 Squadron. Two Belgium pilots, Pilot Officers de Spirlet and Malengreau, were posted to No 56 Squadron as language problems were interfering with night interceptions. Johnny Cock went to No 2 Central Flying School and Ken Tait went to No 56 OTU.

Roddy Rayner was fortunate to catch sight of an He 111, caught in a searchlight beam over Bath on 24 November. Rayner was able to fire a six second burst before the bomber dived away and was lost. On 24 November, the Squadron moved yet again, to Charmy Down, 10 miles to the west of Colerne, which was another new airfield. Here the squadron personnel weathered a harsh winter as new pilots replaced the many who had been posted away to pass on their experience. There was little to interrupt the boredom, so when, on 3 January, one of the new pilots, Flying Officer Smallwoood, attacked and hit a Ju 88, there was great excitement. This reached a pitch when it was reported that a Ju 88 had crashed in the Mendip Hills and the squadron's intelligence officer made telephone calls all over the area in an effort to confirm the rumour. His efforts were in vain, however, and it was concluded that the report had been made in error.

Fog, snow and ice made conditions almost impossible to operate in, yet still it was expected that the Hurricanes should be up to meet the enemy who continued to operate. On 16 January, a particularly large air raid was made upon

Bristol, against which 12 Hurricanes of No 87 Squadron and three from No 501 Squadron were directed. Despite the large number of both bombers and fighters not a shot was fired, nor an enemy seen even though bombs could be seen exploding on the City below.

The story was repeated on 21 February, when nine Hurricanes attempted to intercept the bombing of Swansea. No bombers were seen and it was fortunate that the Hurricane pilots all returned safely although one of their number flew to Andover before finding a place to land. There seemed to be no end to the patrols, the weather and the searchlight co-operation exercises which were dreamed up every so often.

A comic interlude occured at dusk on 8 March, when a fire was seen in the middle of the flare path. Fearing that a 'plane may have crashed on landing, many ran out to see what had happened and found the flare path lorry had caught fire setting off a drum of Lewis gun ammunition in the heat. Fortunately, little damage was done and the flames quelled, but it was a matter of conjecture whether the amateur fire fighters had directed the extinguishers at each other through design or inexperience!

More amusement was caused, on 13 March, when an unidentified aircraft in distress appeared over Charmy Down and the ground controllers were directed to assist it to land. They were also warned that caution should be exercised lest it turn out to be the enemy. After a first class pyrotechnic display the machine landed safely but remained unidentified. Gleed, the commanding officer, and several others went to investigate. As they approached cautiously one of the figures approached Gleed and his band and began to offer an explanation of their arrival in a foreign tongue. Amongst the facts that could be made out were that they had come from Hamburg, which caused further consternation until it was seen that the men were Polish. Just then the bomb doors opened and a large cylinder fell out with a resounding clang which again caused pulses to quicken before it was explained away as a supply container. Back at the dispersal, news was eagerly awaited as to whether the visitor was friend or foe. The question seemed to have been answered when a brief burst of machine gun fire was heard and it was only when Gleed returned that it was learned that someone had decided to empty the guns by the most direct method possible.

On 14 March, orders were received to send two pilots to the Luftwaffe airfield of Capricoquet, near Caen to execute one of the first of the RAF's intruder sorties. The squadron had made several requests to carry out such a mission but only now was it permitted. Once again, Gleed records the night he flew with 'Roddy' Rayner, in his book.

One afternoon Group 'phoned me and said that two air-

Gleed and Rayner in March, 1941 (Watson).

craft were to carry out an offensive patrol and ground straff. They were to be at ———, (Warmwell) one of the 'dromes on the coast, by 18.00 hours, where further instructions and maps would be forthcoming. I said they would be there.

'Robbie (Rayner), I want to talk to you a second. Tonight there's a special job to do. A blitz of an aerodrome on the other side. Would you like to come?'

'Rather, Widge. What's the form?'

'We are to be at ——— by six this evening. We'll get all the dope from the intelligence officer there. We must get flares put in the 'planes, carry revolvers and port flares, just in case we do have to land the other side. If you do, put a couple of bullets in the petrol tank, then shove a port fire in it. That should make a 'plane burn OK.'

'That's grand, Widge. What time shall we leave?' — 'About five fifteen. Fix it up that the 'planes are absolutely OK. Tell Watty that he will be in charge in your absence. We'll be landing back at ——— after the show and staying the night there. — Blast! I'm wanted on the 'phone.' — 'Hullo! Yes, Opps. Two reserves from ''B'' Flight. OK; we'll meet them there at six. Cheerio.'

'Opps say that Group have ordered two of ''B'' Flight to come as reserve. They might go across when we get back.' — 'I wonder where on earth we are going. It's a hell of a way over the sea.' — 'Come down and have a swift tea. We'll tell Mrs Riggers that we'll be out tonight. Hope the weather stays fine.'

We hurtle down to the lovely Cotswold village; there is something gloriously soothing about houses built with the Cotswold stone. I felt the old sinking feeling at the thought of action again. At the least it means a 100 miles of sea out and back. I wonder what their ground defence will be like. Still, it's no damned good worrying.

We have a grand tea — lots of toast, and some of our hostess' home-made jam. Then up to the 'drome. The 'planes are all set. Watty, Dickie and the boys wish us good luck, and beg that they may go next time. I clamber into my mighty 'A'. Then off. The visibility is extremely good: within a few minutes of taking off I could see the sea glinting

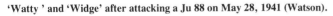
'Watty' and 'Widge' after attacking a Ju 88 on May 28, 1941 (Watson).

silver in the sun, the coastline from the Isle of Wight to Plymouth. It was a marvellous day.

We landed, and were met by the intelligence officer, who had maps for us. Our destination was Caen, an aerodrome east of Cherbourg Peninsula. 135 miles − 130 of those across the sea. 260 miles there and back. Whew! hell of a long swim if anything went wrong.

The intelligence officer unrolled a hugh mosaic photograph − a beautiful piece of work showing every detail. We crowd round and peer at it. 'There's the 'drome; it's six miles from the coast. You can easily recognise it from the railway running parallel to the coast on the southern boundary. You should also be able to see that triangle of roads just west of the 'drome. As you can see, it is an extremely large 'drome; as far as we know, there are dispersal points all round it. The hangars are on the south-east side. Those huts are only wooden; they are worth having a few shots in them. This photo was taken about two months ago, so there may be more huts. If you look carefully, you can see gun-pits − there, there, and there. They are probably pom-poms, like our Bofor guns. I'm afraid we don't know much about their defence at the moment. You should be able to tell us a lot about that when you get back, so try to remember where the gun-posts are. According to our latest information, there is no heavy flak.'

'The object of this raid is to destroy aircraft landing there or parked on the 'drome. They use that 'drome for their returning bombers. You should find something to pot at.'

'I think that is all I can tell you, sir. Here are some escaping kits. Group orders are that you are to take off at midnight, unless they give any order to the contrary. Now I'll take you along to the mess.'

We met in the watch office, 'phoned up the Met office and working out a course. At last everything was fixed. I 'phoned Opps and checked that we were still to go at midnight. They told me to have the aircraft airborne by midnight. RT silence to be maintained on the outward journey. Can be used for homing on the way back. Another half-hour to go.

We sat around kicking our heels, each collecting his parachute and quietly studying the map of the target. It should be very easy to find. Thirty minutes' flying at economical speed. That should give us a safe 20 minutes over there.

'Robbie, we'll get over the 'drome at 12,000, then throttle back and glide down. Start your beat up on the south side. I'll look after the northern half.'

'OK, Widge. If they have got any searchlights, I'll shoot them out if they get on you, and you shoot them out if they get on me.'

'Right. Now don't stay longer than 20 minutes. On the way home give me a call on the RT. You know the form if you are going in the "drink". Scream on the RT and keep calling, to give the ground station a chance to get a fix on you.'

'Right, old boy.'

The telephone rang, and made me, at any rate, jump. 'It's for you, sir.' − 'Hullo! Met. Right. Hold on a second and I'll get a pencil. OK. Now let's have it. Thanks, Met; that's fine.'

'Well, boys, the weather looks OK. I'm not too keen on the sound of the weather later on here. If it duffs up,* Derek, give us a shower of Verey lights to show us the way to come home.' − 'I'll keep a damned good eye on it.' − 'Blast it! I hope it doesn't pack in before we go. What's the time?'

'Twenty-two twelve.'

'Let's go out at quarter to start up at ten to. I'm going to run my engine up damn well first, and make sure that it's OK.'

'I'll get mine started, too,' Bea said. 'Just in case one of your machines is duff.'†

'OK, Bea; thanks a lot. Where the hell are my gloves? Blast! I've left my torch behind. Lend me one, somebody. − Thanks, Derek; I'll give it you as soon as I land. Well, I think we'll wander out.'

We stepped out into the night. What a night! Much more fitting for romance. Still, it couldn't be more perfect for our job.

'Well, good luck, Robbie.'

'Good luck, Widge; don't forget to call me on the way home.'

'I won't.'

'Good luck, sir.' Bea yells as he trots to his machine.

'Good hunting, Widge. Give them hell. Wish I was coming with you now; this waiting browns me off.'

'Thanks, Derek. We'll go together next time, I hope. Don't forget the firework display.'

'I won't; see you in about an hour thirty after take off. Cheerio.'

I clambered into the mighty 'A', turned on the cockpit lights, and strapped myself in with the help of one of the men.

'OK. I'll start up now.'

The engine started at once. I glanced across to Robbie's machine − his engine started OK, too. On with the compass light. I set the course on.

Put gloves on; check position of revolver and port-flares. Give a short puff into the tube of Mae West, just to make sure it is OK. I feel it swell. That's OK. The engine temperatures slowly crawl up their gauges. I open the throttle full. Revs OK. Test the mags. Slight drop. That's OK. I throttle back. Turn on the reflector sight and turn it down to dim. That should be OK. I look across and see Robbie silhouetted in his cockpit. It is five to twelve. I give him the thumbs-up sign. He returns it. OK. Slowly I taxi out. As I do so I glance at the stars. The aeroplanes dispersed round the 'drome show up shining silver in the moonlight. If there is anything to see, we should most certainly see it tonight.

The coast was a lovely sight, the calm sea reflecting the moon. Every little boat was visible. We climbed slowly upwards. The coast had receded out of sight behind us by the time we were at 12,000. It was incredibly lovely looking at the silver sea. After a glance at the instruments, I turned all the cockpit lights out except the compass light. We levelled out at 12,000, and throttled even farther back.

'Christ! there it is' − the 'drome with a square wood at one corner. It looks a terrific light patch: just like its photo that we had seen on the mosaic map. To the east a white beacon is blinking the letter B. I throttle back even more. The 'drome, like the town, is completely without lights. Six thousand feet now. Nothing happens. The hangars stand up well; we are still too high to see any aircraft. The huts show up well now. There are about double the number that there had been on the photo. Two thousand feet. There they are. A neat row of twin-engined 'planes; another row. What are they? Junkers 88s. 'Hell! and 215s.' I waggle my wings − the sign for Robbie to break away. At 1,000 feet I shove the throttle full open. That line of about nine will do me nicely. A steep right-hand turn. Now down. Sights on. Steady. I thumb the firing-button. A stream of fire pours from my wings; back on the stick, the line of aircraft flash through my sights. 'Hell! pom poms.' A string of fiery ping-pong balls tear by my wings; another stream; then another. 'Oh, Hell! searchlights.' Four blue searchlights leap out of the shadows. 'Blast! they've got me.' My wings are suddenly shining a brilliant silver. 'Head in cockpit, quick!' I yank

---

* "Duffs up" means becomes thick with either low cloud or ground haze.
† And, by extension, anything which goes wrong.

back on the stick. 'Steady. Robbie, pull your finger out and shoot them off me. Thank God I'm clear of them now.' — 'Christ!' a glance behind shows me a stream of pom-pom shells seemingly appearing from a circle round the 'drome, all meeting in an apex. 'Oh God!' For a fleeting second I catch a glimpse of a 'Hurribird' caught in the searchlights surrounded by snacky iridescent shells. 'You bastards!' I pull up into a steep left-hand turn. 'Look out! you'll be coming out of the moon. Oh, blast the moon! Here goes.' I come in low. 'There they are.' Another line of aircraft. Brrrrrmmmm, brrrmmmmmmmm. 'Damn those search-lights!' One is shining from straight in front of me. I fly straight at it. Brrrrrmmmmm, brrrrrrm. 'Got you!' For a second there is a red glow, then the searchlight goes out. 'One more dive and I've had enough. Christ, those pom-poms are hell. Brmmmmm, hissssssshissssss. Blast! out of ammo. Home, and don't spare the horses.'

I roar over Caen, just missing the church spire. 'You b———s!' From the street corners and the windows of houses little flickers of light flash. rifle and revolver fire. Back with the stick. I zoom up to 2,000 feet. 'Christ! there goes Robbie.' A shower of pom-pom shells snake across the 'drome behind me. No searchlights are on now, and not so many guns are firing. 'Cockpit lights on. Christ! radiator temperature 120; oil pressure OK. Oil temperature 75. Keep cool! That's all right. It's not up to the emergency temperature. Throttle back, you fool! before the engine does blow up. I pulled the throttle back and shoved her in weak mixture. 'Now petrol. Port tank ten gallons, starboard slightly less than ten. That's not too bad. Gravity tank full. Phew! it's hot. My clothes are dripping with sweat.'

I crossed the French coast, climbing slowly, steadied up on my homeward course. 'Keep that star just on the edge of the windscreen and that will be OK. Thank God I'm still alive. What's the time? Twelve forty-seven. Christ, is that all? Now call Robbie on the RT.' — 'Hullo, Robbie! Widge calling. Are you OK? Over.' — Nothing. I wait a minute. Except for the crackle of atmospherics not a sound comes through the RT. — 'Hullo, Robbie! Hullo, Yellow 1! Are you OK? Over.' — Nothing. 'Oh, please God, what has happened to him? How can I explain it to his girl friend? Perhaps he has force-landed and is all right.' — 'Hullo, Robbie! are you receiving? Over.' . . . Still nothing. The engine seems to be running rough, the temperatures are lower now. 'Perhaps I've got a bullet in the radiator. Oh God, don't let me drop in the sea. What shall I tell the boys about Robbie? Oh, why did we ever start on this show? Don't be a fool! Robbie may be perfectly OK, except his radio has packed. But it was all right when he tested it. God, where are you, Robbie?'

I glance at the clock. One o'clock: halfway. 'If I fall in "the drink" now I haven't a hope of being picked up. I'll shoot myself before we hit. — No, don't be a fool; while there's life there's hope. I can't stand floating about; if I drop in I'll shoot myself.' Another 10 minutes. I peer through the windscreen. 'Hell! clouds below me. Stay up above them: if your engine cuts, you'll need every foot of height.' Beneath me there was about 7/10s* cloud. Another five minutes. 'Except for this blasted cloud, I could very likely see the coast. It's wonderful to be alive.' Ten past one. Time to go beneath the cloud. 'Turn on to gravity: the wing-tanks are just about empty.' I throttle back and glide down. The tops of the clouds look like snowy mountains shining in the moon. Soon I was enveloped in the white misty clouds. Thank God they weren't thick. I came out of them at 2,000. 'Thank God, there's the coast. Now where the hell am I?' I cross the coast. 'Good old England! God, how pleased I am to see you! There's the beacon. Oh, good

The ground crew pose on an extremely battered Hurricane night fighter in May 1941 (Martin).

old Derek!' A green Verey light soars up. 'There's the 'drome.' I turn on the navigation lights and roar around the 'drome; the green aldis lamp winks at me from the flare-path. 'Wheels down, flaps down, into land. Bump, bump.'

Dark figures jump up on to my wing.

'How did you get on, Widge?'

'OK, Derek. Is Robbie back yet?'

'No.'

'Did you find it easily, Widge? What were the 'planes on the deck?' Bea asked.

'It was a piece of cake finding the 'drome. The course was damned good: we arrived the other side about a mile too far west. The 'planes were 88s, 109s and I think some Dornier 215s: parked in beautiful straight lines. Christ! I wish Robbie would hurry up. Sshhhhh! do you hear an engine?'

'It sounds like a "Hurribird"; let's sling up a Verey light.'

'OK, Widge, I've got it here,' said Derek.

Crack! A green light soars up.

'There he is; thank God for that!'

The intelligence officers turned up, and helped us write out our reports. Then, after a marvellous cup of tea, bed. I lay in bed and thought. I wondered how many Huns we had killed that night: where on earth the Jerries had got all the guns from. Thank God for getting us home safely. We must win this war soon.''

Bad weather thwarted interception attempts during a raid on Bristol on 16 March. As conditions worsened the three Hurricane pilots were recalled to Charmy Down where they joined the circuit with a Wellington, a Blenheim and Beaufighter, all of which had been caught out by the weather. To add to the confusion, several bombs intended for Bristol, but jettisoned over the only lights visible, fell near the flare path. Eventually all six machines came down safely although the Beaufighter overshot and 'piled up' in a field at the end of the runway. A few days later two Hurricane pilots also overshot and ended up in the same field, giving the airfield the appearance of a salvage dump.

The next major raid on Bristol came on 3 April, when Flight Lieutenant Carver was one of those on patrol. Seeing his target ahead, Carver began his approach and was greeted by a display of incorrect recognition signals which further confused matters, but as control believed it to be hostile he opened fire. The aircraft took fire and crashed to the ground near Sturminster Newton. Tragically it was discovered that the bomber was a Whitley, from No 51 Squadron, which had been returning from a raid on Germany. Only one of the five crew members baled out safely.

Three pilots, Flight Lieutenant Ward, Pilot Officer Beamont and Flight Sergeant Badger were sent to Exeter to operate from there on 4 April. At dusk, three Ju 88s flew low over Exeter and released their bombs just as the pilots ran to their Hurricanes. One bomb fell so close to Flight Sergeant Badger that he was flung against a wall by the blast which injured his back so badly that he spent the next three weeks in hospital. The remaining two pilots gave chase, but returned after a long chase through cloud with the news that they may have damaged one of the bombers.

Three nights later, while still based at Exeter, Flight Lieutenant Ward saw a bright glow in the sky at 10,000 and took a pop shot at it as it fell past him. It was later learned that it was an He 111 of 9/KG26 which had been engaged by the famous Squadron Leader Cunningham in a Beaufighter of No 604 Squadron and had fallen into the sea off Branscombe, Devon.

A repeat attack on Caen − Carpiquet Airfield was made by Flight Lieutenant Ward and Pilot Officer Beamont on 14 March. Although no flying was in progress, the Hurricane pilots shot at two parked aircraft, buildings and a train leaving Caen Station, which was left in clouds of steam and smoke.

After many months with little to show for their efforts, the squadron were rewarded with the credit for the destruction of an He 111 which crashed on the Isle of Wight on 10 April. Roddy Rayner made an interception over Gloucester and chased the bomber to Portsmouth, making seven attacks during which he exhausted his ammunition. The following night another large raid was directed at Bristol, but this time a full moon aided location and several bombers were even seen from the ground and one flew so low over the airfield that the Lewis gun crew fired on it. Both 'A' and 'B' Flights were airborne but only one pilot, Pilot Officer Musgrove, engaged the enemy which he left losing height rapidly some 20 miles out to sea.

In addition to their nocturnal activities, the squadron continued their patrol activities over the Channel and acted as air cover to shipping convoys. Sergeant Stirling was reported missing from one such sortie on 12 April and was assumed to have fallen into the sea and drowned. Two days later, a report was received that a German coastal patrol had picked Stirling up from the sea off the French Coast and had taken him prisoner.

The April moon which had given some prospect of interception was on the wane and reduced the already meagre

Alex Thom with his ground crew, far right is Reg Guppy. The aircraft is one of the cannon-armed 11Cs which came into service in 1941 (Guppy).

chances of interception. Fifteen Hurricanes were ordered up on 15 April but no interceptions were made which lead the squadron adjutant to write:

''In spite of great keenness and optimism, it looks as if the squadron have before them some weeks of searching for a black needle in a black haystack in the blackout before next month's moon arrives.''

During the latter part of April and early May, this prediction was realised, there being little for the squadron's pilots to engage. A strange order was, however, given to Flying Officer 'Watty' Watson on the night of 4 May.

''I was standing at available at Charmy Down, when it was reported that a hostile aircraft was almost overhead. I went outside and saw it, and took off in pursuit. I was vectored behind, and after 15−20 minutes flying I saw AA fire off Portland and a little later saw the bandit at 8,000 feet ahead being attacked by a Spitfire from the port quarter and drawing return fire form the bandit, as I approached I noticed that the bandit looked like a Whitley and later confirmed this. The markings were very indistinct and there were no tail markings, nor were any recognition signals given. I informed control of the fact and was told to engage. I fired one burst of approx. 100 yards from each gun in a quarter from port. The Spitfire doing the same. Another Spitfire attacked from starboard and the engine caught fire, and the bandit winged over towards the sea, where it spun in and crashed. It went under and left only air bubbles and a patch of burning oil.''

The aircraft crashed into the sea 25 miles south of Portland at about 06.45 hours and left Watson to wonder what had been going on. When he landed, it became clear that the crew had baled out of the Whitley and left the bomber on 'George', the auto pilot, which seemed intent on heading for occupied France. It was therefore decided to destroy the bomber over the sea.

An intruder sortie to Marpetus was scheduled for the next night, but was cancelled before the pilots took off. The following night, Gleed and Thorogood set off to Marpetus but failed to find it in the poor weather. Undeterred, they set off again on 7 May, but when mid-way across the Channel, Gleed spotted what he identified as a Dornier Do 17 heading in the opposite direction. After four bursts, the bomber's starboard engine caught fire, the flames spread and eventually it pancaked on the sea where it sank. Pilot Officers Beamont and Roscoe did make their way to Marpetus where they shot up several Me 109s parked there and survived the intense flak and machine gun fire.

Two fitters, Richard Martin and Joe Holland, hard at work on a Hurricane (Martin).

44

The 'Hairy' nature of operating from the Scillies landing strip is well conveyed by this snapshot of ground crew assisting a Hurricane to turn at St. Mary's in the limited area available (Martin).

The ground crews head for the Scillies on board the *The Scillonian*. 'Chiefy' Knopp is in the centre of this group (Martin).

7. And so to the Scillies

The area off the south-western tip of England, the Western Approaches and the Irish Sea were, at this stage of the war, considered by the Luftwaffe a comparatively 'safe' area. Most of this expanse of sea was beyond the range of home based fighters, but if a base could be established on the Scilly Isles, Fighter Command considered that at least some of the 'gap' could be covered. Of the 140 or so rocky islands which make up the Scilly Isles, only six are habitable and only one, St Mary's, boasted anything resembling a landing strip. It had been used by a local airline in pre-war days for landing de Havilland Rapide biplanes, but as to whether a high performance machine such as the Hurricane could land safely on the 450 yards of grass, that was another matter.

To prove the practicality of the idea, an area approximating to that of the island landing ground was marked out at Charmy Down and all of No 87 Squadron's pilots landed successfully on it. All being well, six Hurricanes, flown by Squadron Leader 'Widge' Gleed, 'Roddy' Rayner, 'Bea' Beamont, 'Watty' Watson, Pilot Officer Badger and Sergeant 'Rubber' Thorogood, set out for St Mary's on 19 May, for what became known as a 'fishing expedition.'

As the pilots circled the landing strip it looke. smaller than ever. There was a distinct bump in the middle, rocks on the coastal side and a fir tree plantation on the other. Skill was required to get down in one piece and to control the landing run which was hampered by the difficulty in breaking on the wet grass. 'Widge' Gleed made the first attempt at landing, he got down alright but used most of the 450 yards to stop. The others, spurred on by his success, also landed safely. The groundcrew at once set about re-fuelling the aircraft. The pilots hardly had time to congratulate themselves on their landings when, at 21.00 hours, a visual signal from a local coastguard station, in the shape of a red flare, indicated an aeroplane just south of the islands. The only Hurricanes ready and in position for take off were 'Widge' Gleed's and Pilot Officer Badger's, they quickly climbed into their cockpits and were off.

Badger sighted his prey five miles south of St Mary's and flying at less than 200 feet. He identified it as an He 114 but it was acturally an Arado Ar 196 from the reconnaissance unit 5/196, being flown by Leutnant Karl Schmidt. As Badger approached, Schmidt jettisoned his bomb load and headed south while taking evasive action by turning left and right. At 200 yards Badger opened fire and closed to just 50 yards as he fired three more bursts which caused the floatplane to turn steeply to the right and break up as it hit the sea.

Still in the Scilly Isles, 'Widge' Gleed and 'Rubber' Thorogood were returning from an unsuccessful patrol to the north of the islands on 24 May. As the pilots made their final approaches, with flaps and wheels in the down position, the front gunner of an aircraft which was identified as a Dornier Do 18 opened fire as it passed overhead. Gleed and Thorogood made repeated attacks which eventually produced a small fire in the cockpit area and the machine began a left hand turn down to the sea. As it hit the sea, the flyingboat broke up and began to burn leaving a rising column of black smoke as the only reminder. As the two pilots returned to St Mary's, Thorogood noticed that the airspeed indicator of his Hurricane had failed which lead to problems on landing at the small strip when he struck a small rock and damaged an oleo leg and the airscrew.

The final aciton of this 'fishing expedition' came on 28 May, when 'Widge' Gleed and 'Watty' Watson attacked a Ju 88 to the south of the islands. Although repeated attacks were made by both pilots and the port engine of the bomber was put out of action, it was not seen to crash and was therefore claimed as a shared 'probable'. The pilots returned to Charmy Down at the end of May and during June, two more 'fishing expeditions' were made but without success.

Despite the poor quality of this rare snapshot, the main buildings at St. Mary's can be seen, two small huts, with Hurricanes parked at the edge of the airstrip.

When the squadron made their next visit to the Scilly Isles, in July 1941, Gleed, with the squadron adjutant, Flight Lieutenant John Strachey, set about organising things and obtained two field telephones which were linked to observation points such as coastguard look-outs and the Bishop's Rock Lighthouse. The pattern of operations was for two Hurricanes to be prepared at readiness with their pilots in the cockpits awaiting the scramble signal of a red flare to be fired from the telephone hut. When airborne, detials of the enemy's height and bearing would be given over the RT.

Whilst the overall attitude of the native islanders was one of welcome and kindness, some had reservations as to the safety of their daughters. Tea and cakes were often brought to the pilots as they sat at readiness and huge quantities of scones, cream, butter, cheese and flowers were available to those that wanted them. A favourite perk for the pilots was to load the produce into the rear of ones Hurricane when flying back to the mainland. Of course, it was all intended 'for their mothers' but not a little mysteriously found its way onto the Black Market. Accommodation for officers and NCOs was found in the many vacant guest houses of the peace-time holiday resort but to begin with the groundcrews were less well catered for and given tents to erect on the airfield.

The next opportunity for action came on 18 July, when Flying Officer Roscoe and Sergeant Thom were alerted to the presence of an He 111, flying low and to the west of St Agnes. Sergeant Alex Thom closed to 150 yards and with two short bursts disabled the bomber's starboard engine, leaving a trail of oil and glycol in its wake which covered Thom's windscreen. As he tried to clear the oil away using the screen de-icing fluid, Roscoe made further attacks until, with a final series of attacks from both pilots, the Heinkel 'pancaked' on the sea. The crew of four broke out the dinghy and pushed off, leaving the bomber to sink whilst Thom circled overhead and Roscoe went back to St Mary's to summon the assistance of a motor launch to pick up the

crew. Some 35 miles south-south-west of St Agnes, the bomber's crew were picked up after spending 1½ hours in their dinghy. Upon interrogation it was found that they were from 2/KG 28 and had been engaged on an anti-shipping sortie when intercepted. The pilot, Leutnant Ernst Thiele, had taken off in the He 111 coded IT+FK from Nantes with two 500 kg bombs on board but had failed to locate any targets and was returning from a patrol between the Scillies and Pembroke. He attributed the loss of his aircraft to the incompetence of the Luftwaffe's meteorological service, which had forecast low cloud on a day which turned out to be bright and sunny.

The reduction in the scale of operations by the Luftwaffe during late July and August was reflected in the lack of interceptions made either from the Scilly Isles or Charmy Down. Countless friendly aircraft of all shapes and sizes were encountered during patrols and searchlight co-operation flights provided practice for their operators, but proved particularly irksome for the pilots involved. In early August, 'Widge' Gleed made a test flight in a new version of the Hurricane, the Hurricane IIC, which was armed with four 20 mm cannon in place of the usual eight 0.303 inch Browning machine guns. A tank was the target for the practice attack and was, rather satisfyingly, set on fire with a short burst from the battery of cannon.

An intruder operation to Marpetus Airfield was scheduled for the night of 6 August. Gleed and Thorogood went to the newly opened airfield of Ibsley, near Ringwood in Hampshire, where they joined forces with Group Captain Hope who had been a long term friend of the squadron's personnel. On their arrival over the airfield the only aircraft visible were two Me 109s which were duly shot up on the ground. Return light anti-aircraft fire was intense and, as Gleed and Thorogood left the target, a red flash and fire was seen on the ground. Group Captain Hope did not return and the sad conclusion was reached that the flash must have been made by his Hurricane as it crashed. Subsequently it was learned via the Red Cross that a 'Pilot Officer Hope' with the correct initials and identity number had been killed at this time.

The following day the squadron moved to Colerne, where the personnel once more began to make their home in new surroundings. Within a few days of the move, on the night of August 10th, 1941, four Hurricanes took part in a co-operation exercise with 'Turbinlite' Havocs of No 1454 Flight. The trials involved a Havoc fitted with airborne interception equipment 'AI' and a large searchlight in the nose. The concept had been dreamed up by Air Commodore A E Clouston, who had made his name in pre-war days as a record breaking pilot in aircraft such as the de Haviland 'Comet' racer, as a stop-gap night fighter to make up for the lack of AI (Radar) equipped night fighters. Sergeant Jack Harding was one of the pilots who flew on this 'amusing and hairy' flight:

Ken Hughes has lunch at St. Mary's in May, 1941. The 'table' is the crate in which Thorogood's new propeller blades were shipped following his crash landing on May 25. Hughes started an airfreight business after the war and developed his company to become one of the largest carriers in Great Britain. (Watson).

"The idea was that the Havoc took off at night with a Hurricane formating on each wing tip. The three aircraft were then directed by a ground control station 'GCI' onto the target aircraft. The flying called for all three aircraft to keep tightly together, through thick cloud if necessary. Once the target was judged to be in range, one of the Hurricanes was instructed to attack and some seconds after going forward the light would be switched on to illuminate the target. The second Hurricane would then go forward also, to 'finish off' the bandit.

Such was the theory! In practice, the first thing that the lead Hurricane found was the slipstream of the target, then he was blinded by the brilliant light from behind obscuring the windscreen. There then followed a series of involuntary aerobatics terminating several thousand feet below, each Hurricane looking for the black Havoc in a very black sky.''

After many months of fruitless trials and attempted interceptions, the whole project was abandoned and the aircraft converted back to their standard configuration.

A detachment on the Scilly Isles was alerted by the coastguards to two bandits flying at fifty feet north-west of the Bishop's Rock Lighthouse, on 16 August. Pilot Officer 'Kit' Forsyth scrambled at 17.05 hours and chased what he identified as two Ju 88s at full boost for 15 minutes. The pair broke up and Forsyth singled out one, the rear gunner of which returned fire. After several attacks at sea level first the starboard and then the port engine caught fire, the port wing seemed to explode and then fell off, leaving the bomber to crash into the sea and sink without trace.

Whilst still on the Scilly Isles, on 26 August, a lone bomber flew over St Mary's and dropped his bombs on the town. There were two casualties, both young women, one of whom was Miss Jenkins, who had looked after the airmen billeted in her house for many months. Pilot Officer Musgrove was the first to scramble and, after some difficulty in the failing light, identified a Ju 88 flying east at 2,000 feet. After several attacks, flames and sparks were

A Turbinlite Havoc similar to those that the squadron attempted to follow at night.

coming from the bomber's starboard engine but Musgrove was forced to break off his attack as he had exhausted his ammunition, it was nevertheless considered as destroyed.

In recent months, the squadron had been fortunate in that they had lost no pilots in accidents or combat. Tragedy struck on the night of 3 September, the second anniversary of the outbreak of war, when Sergeant Loughridge crashed during a night flying exercise and was killed. Later in the month, on the 26th, Sergeant Edwards misjudged a practice ground attack exercise at Doddington and died in the resulting crash. Flying Officer Shimmons, while flying on a 'Turbinlite' Havoc patrol over Devon on the night of 1 October, announced over the RT that he was having engine trouble and was going to bale out. This he managed but was slightly injured, his Hurricane, now left to its own devices crashed into the sea off the coast.

After many weeks of practice flights an operational patrol with a 'Turbinlite' Havoc took place on the night of 6 October. Squadron Leader Carver and 'Watty' Watson chased after the enemy for 20 minutes but owing to the lack of speed of the Havoc, just over 300 Knots, he could not be caught. The next night the story was repeated as it was to be by other squadrons throughout the country over the coming months.

'Rubber' Thorogood, now one of the longest serving of the squadron's pilots and promoted to the rank of Pilot Officer, was forced to bale out of his Hurricane on the night of 14 October. Save for hurting a foot, Thorogood landed safely whilst his Hurricane crashed into a hedgerow and burst into flames only yards from houses in the village of Beanacre. This incident entitled 'Rubber' to the Bar to his Caterpillar Club Badge for taking to his parachute for a second time. Pilot Officer Musgrove also injured himself this night when he executed a forced landing on the Scilly Isles and was taken to hospital.

Opportunity for combat returned to the detachment based on the Scilly Isles when, on 20 October, Pilot Officer Jewell and Sergeant Thom scrambled to intercept an He 111 which had been spotted by the Vigilant St Agnes coastguards. Only Thom located his target which he set about with a series of astern attacks which silenced the rear gunners and allowed him to close to point blank range until both engines had been severely damaged and his ammunition exhausted. Unable to inflict any further damage, Thom followed the bomber for a few minutes before he returned to base to claim the Heinkel as 'probably destroyed'. Although it cannot be confirmed, it is possible that Thom's victim was one of the two He 111s of III/KG 40 which failed to return from sorties off the west coast of England.

Sergeant Thom was also involved in the following day's combat when he and the recovered Pilot Officer Musgrove

A line-up of immaculately turned out Hurricane IIs at Charmy Down in December 1941 (Harding).

set off to intercept an Me 110 reported by the St Martin's coastguards. The Me 110, from 3/(F)123, was engaged on a maritime reconnaissance sortie and was found flying at just 50 feet some 30 miles south-east of the islands. Musgrove, after a hopeful 'long drop' burst from over a mile range closed to 200 yards and made a firing pass to 50 yards which silenced Unteroffizier Kirchenbauer, the rear gunner. Thom then caused black smoke to belch from the Messerschmitt's port engine and then both pilots made further attacks which put the other engine out of action and the Me 110 pancaked into the sea. Feldwebel Otto Eberl, the pilot, was seen struggling free and although he had a life jacket his aircraft sank before the dinghy could be released. Seeing the plight the enemy found himself in, Musgrove succeeded in unstowing his own dinghy and throwing it down to Eberl, but it seemed to land some distance away and he may not have been able to reach it. A Naval launch was summoned from Falmouth, but this failed to locate the unfortunate pilot whose body was washed ashore near Barnstaple nearly two months later.

A further series of accidents overtook the squadron in the next few weeks. The commanding officer, Squadron Leader 'Widge' Gleed, was the first victim when he was compelled to force land an Airacobra which he was test flying. He escaped without injury, as did Sergeant Norsham who baled out of his Hurricane when its engine failed, he landed in a tree but managed to untangle himself. Sergeants Gallus and Beda collided when on a 'Turbinlite' Havoc co-operation flight on the night of 26 October, both pilots baled out safely and landed near the village of East Knowle.

The worsening winter weather permitted little flying during November, the principal event of the month being the posting of 'Widge' Gleed, now Wing Commander Ian Gleed DFC, to Wing Commander (Flying) at Middle Wallop. His place as commanding officer was taken by Squadron Leader Smallwood, who had previously flown

The squadron's officers gather for a photograph in front of *Cawnpore I*. Left to right; F/O Cohlan, P/O Lewis, F/O Gorzula, S/Ldr Smallwood, P/O Jewell, F/Lt Roscoe, and F/O Strachey (adjutant) (Harding).

with the squadron as a flight commander. December brought little cheer for the squadron. On the 13th, a Canadian pilot who had been with the squadron for just over one month, Sergeant Robinson, spun and lost control of his Hurricane when flying in cloud over Bristol. Whether he chose to stay with his machine or could not bale out is unknown, but his Hurricane dived almost vertically into the ground at Morebrook Farm, near the village of Almondsbury.

Much amusement was had at the expense of Flight Lieutenant Roscoe, during the afternoon of 16 December. He set off eagerly to do battle with a runaway balloon but as dusk fell and the prey appeared increasingly bright it was realised that it was Venus and he was forced to abandon his interesting but fruitless chase. Sergeant Jack Harding also had a most memorable happening the same day when he was asked to test fly a Hurricane which had been delivered the previous day:

"Just after becoming airborne, the starboard wing began to drop which no movement of the stick could correct. Looking down at the base of the control column, I could see that the aileron chain had snapped and the operating rod had fallen onto the cockpit floor. By this time the aircraft was trying to turn turtle, so I grabbed the rods to bring the aircraft back into level flight very close to the ground. After trying various tactics at a safe height, as no radio had been fitted at the time, I decided to have a go at landing. The problem was that if I held the rods to keep the wing up, my head was well below cockpit level and I couldn't see out. If I let the rods go, the wing dropped sharply. By dint of alternatively crouching down and stretching up, a safe landing was made. There was a tragic ending to this story; That same day the Hurricane had a new aileron chain fitted and during the evening it was taken up, by Sergeant Ray Chivers, on a night flying exercise. Shortly after take off the engine cut and the Hurricane ploughed into an adjoining hillside, killing Ray. The cause of the 'prang' was never discovered."

Christmas Eve turned out to be one of the clearest nights of the year, which was unfortunate for the duty pilots as both searchlight and Havoc co-operation flights were made. The weather turned foul on Christmas Day itself and all were able to celebrate well into the night knowing that they would not be called upon to fly. The next day a posting came for 'Watty' Watson, he was to report to the Gloucester Aircraft Company for test pilot's duties.

'Watty' was, by this time, the longest serving pilot with No 87 Squadron and with his leaving ended an episode in the history of the squadron. It is, therefore, a fitting place to end the story of this Hurricane Squadron's hardest years.

Lawrence 'Rubber' Thorogood, continued to fly operations over Europe after leaving No 87 Squadron and rose to the rank of Squadron Leader. After leaving the RAF, 'Rubber' took up a Government post in London and has retired to Cambridgeshire.

Denis Smallwood, now Air Chief Marshall Sir Dennis Smallwood, GBE, KCB,DSO,DFC pursued a most successful career in the RAF and later with British Aerospace for which he was knighted.

Herbert Walton, Alex Thom, David Rodgers, Jack Harding and Tommy Thompson all survived the war and have retired to various parts of Britain from which they travel to attend the annual reunions.